AN INTRODUCTION TO ISLAMIC ECONOMICS

AN INTRODUCTION TO ISLAMIC ECONOMICS

Muhammad Akram Khan

KITAB BHAVAN
New Delhi -2 [India]

AN INTRODUCTION TO ISLAMIC ECONOMI

KITAB BHAVAN

Publishers, Distributors, Exporters & Importers
1784, Kalan Mahal, Darya Ganj,
New Delhi - 1100 02 (India)

Phones : (91-11) 23277392/93, 23274686, 32906
Fax : (91-11) 23263383

Website : www.kitabbavan.net
: www.kitabbavan.com

Email : nasri@vsnl.com
: nusrat@bol.net.in

1st Published in India : 1999
3rd Edition : 2014

ISBN : 81-7151-263-1
Book Code No. : I00344

Printed & Published in India by :
Nusrat Ali Nasri for KITAB BHAVAN
1784, Kalan Mahal, Darya Ganj,
New Delhi - 1100 02 [India]

CONTENTS

LIST OF FIGURES

LIST OF TABLES

FOREWORD

Although Islamic Economics is still in its early stages of development as an academic discipline, there is a constant flow of useful and valuable literature on its different aspects and themes relating to Islam's economic teachings. There is also a rich scholarly tradition from whose womb this nascent discipline has emerged. In all ages and times Muslim scholars have written on the economic teachings of Islam. The current century has, however, been particularly prolific. Theologians, legists, *fuqahā'*, social thinkers and reformers have profusely written on economic themes and have tried to identify what guidance could be drawn from the Islamic sources—the Qur'ān, *Sunnah, Fiqh,* social thought and historical experience. Lurid light has been thrown on certain aspects, like prohibition of *ribā,* dynamic potential of *zakāt*, concept of property and enterprise, role of state, etc. Reflection and discussion continue on many more aspects from the micro level to the global issues. It is in the context of this rich intellectual background that the Muslim economists are trying to develop what can be described as 'Islamic Economics'.

There is also an increasing realisation that Islamic economics cannot be studied in isolation—it can seek flowering only in the context of a whole social system. Contemporary Muslim economists have, on the one hand, gone deep into the original sources to understand the Islamic ideals and targets and, on the other, to realistically comprehend the process through which the Muslim society is passing i.e. a status quo that is a complex of vestiges of the great historic traditions, polluted and corrupted by a colonial past, during which a host of foreign values, laws, institutions and consequent distortions were imposed upon it. As such the problems of transition are beginning to attract more and more the attention of researchers and scholars.

More fundamental is the debate on the future of the very paradigm of economics. The economic paradigm, which has held the sway for the last two centuries, is not only showing cracks beyond repair; its very theoretical foundations, underlying assumptions and capacities to predict future modes of behaviour, are being challenged. Discussion is no longer confined to changes within the paradigm; the current debate is moving more and more towards the *need for the change of the paradigm itself.* "Challenged", writes Amitai Etzioni, "is the entrenched utilitarian, rationalistic, individualistic, neo-classical paradigm which is applied not merely to the economy but also, increasingly to the full array of social relations, from crion to family" (Amitai Etzioni, *The Moral Dimension: Towards a New Economics,* New York, Macmillan, 1988, p.ix).

The economic paradigm is being challenged at its very core: the neo-classical paradigm does not merely ignore the moral dimension, but actually opposes its inclusion. The new emerging paradigm, on the other hand, visualises assigning "a key role for moral values." Then alone may it be possible, underscores Etzioni, to "seek both what is right and what is pleasurable" (*ibid.,* pp.ix, x). Cristovam Buarque, a well-known Brazilian economist and a former Rector of the University of Barasilia, makes a more dispassionate plea for this new approach to economics in his latest work: *The End of Economics: Ethics and the Disorder of Progress,* translated by Mark Ridd, (London, Zed Books, 1993). The failure of economics lies in ignoring social and ethical values. "Social objectives", he asserts, "have been subordinated and viewed as a consequence of technical progress rather than as the purpose of civilization. Ethical values, meanwhile, have been discarded" (p.xi). What is needed is a fundamental change of approach and a total re-ordering of the priorities. He comes to the conclusion:

> Just as physics stumbled upon the need for regulatory ethics the moment it became aware of its catastrophic potential, so Economics sorely needs to rediscover Ethics. The present dilemma will not be dispelled merely by re-evaluating the means and totting up new costs—as

> one does in project assessment. Rather it is a matter of changing the core objectives of the social process, delivering it from economistic strait-jacket of the last two centuries.
>
> Without subverting the traditional notion of progress, it will be impossible to grapple with the problem of growing poverty and inequality, and impossible to incorporate ecological balance, into social purposes. The issue of economic development thus demands a fresh theoretical approach founded on three pillars: an ethics for redefining the very objectives of civilization; a new definition of the object and field of study, capable of taking in the ecological dimension; and a new rationale for Economics as a discipline (*ibid*., p.xii).

The result of this approach would be that: "Technological options must be determined by an economic rationale subordinate to social objectives formulated by ethical values. The hierarchical order: technical values/economic rationale/social objectives/ethical values, would thus be reversed" (*ibid*., p.164).

Coming to the ground situation of the world economy it deserves to be noted that the socialist economic experiment has miserably failed, while the capitalist economies, despite long strides in the fields of economic growth and technological transformation, are in the throes of an ever-deepening crisis. Modern economy has failed to ensure distributive justice, sustained growth and social harmony for a vast majority of mankind and is confronted at home and abroad with the menaces of prolonged recession, persistent unemployment, stagflation, unrestrained monetary expansions, staggering mountains of domestic and foreign debts, and co-existence of extremes of affluence and stark poverty within as well as among the community of nations. The link between moral values and economic judgement and behaviour, both at individual as well as governmental levels which had sustained humanity through the millenna, had been torn as under during the age of secular capitalistic ascendance and the economists as well as the common man are now trying to re-discover that missing ethical link.

'Islamic economics' represents a systematic effort by Muslim economists to cast a fresh look on the entire economic problem and methodology and come up with fresh solutions to old and persisting problems. We are aware that the Muslim economists have a long way to go, but there is no doubt that a beginning has been made in this direction. This beginning bears great promise for the future.

Brother Mohammad Akram Khan is one of those scholars who have shown keen and persistent interest in Islamic economics. He has already produced an extremely useful annotated bibliography on Islamic economics. He has also written quite extensively on a number of substantive issues, particularly in the fields of banking, performance audit and rural finance. His present study covers a rather vast area, from Islam's world view and basic economic concepts to a number of policy prescriptions. The value of the book lies in its simplicity, directness of style, unapologetic approach and reliance on original sources to develop Islamic perspectives on a number of economic concepts, issues and problems. I am confident that *An Introduction to Islamic Economics* will be of great assistance to the uninitiated reader, particularly for the students of economics. It will help the reader develop familiarity with a large number of issues that go to make up the current matrix of Islamic economics. I welcome the publication of this short but useful book and am also happy to record that its publication marks a new phase in the history of cooperation between the International Institute of Islamic Thought, Washington/Islamabad and the Institute of Policy Studies, Islamabad who have jointly sponsored its publication.

Islamabad
October , 1994

KHURSHID AHMAD

PREFACE

The achievements of the 20th century are too numerous to be counted. However, in the final analysis, the material advancements of this century have concealed from our eyes the persistent despoiling of human qualities and the erosion of the moral bases of human culture. The unprecedented material prosperity that came along with technological developments made available to an ordinary person a lifestyle which used to be the prerogative of kings alone and the elite in the last century. This became possible only with the help the of money that was made available to finance scientific research and large development projects. But unfortunately the entire effort to increase the inventory of material possessions and comforts left out of its focus the most important element — man himself.

The accumulated effort of all nations of the world during the whole century contributed only to the growth and development of human beings as mere cogs in a vast development machine. For man was not conceived as the crown of all development efforts. At best he was treated as 'human capital'. As a result, very little was done for the education and training of man to bring about his cultural advancement and to nurture fellow-feelings in him. Even today, gross disparities exist in the provision of basic services like potable water, sanitation, medical care, roads, fuel gas, electricity and telephones between rural and urban areas and between rich and poor countries, although a lot of lip service has been paid to the equality of human beings. The allocation of resources has been guided mostly by economic and financial criteria and not by human needs. Similarly, the research programmes in science and technology are guided by potential pay-back for business firms or economic power for the state. Capital, wherever it is available, flows to the programmes where it has all the safeguards and an assured return. Financial considerations reign supreme. There are vast spans of undeveloped earth and oceans, and infinite potentialities of development, enough to enrich everyone on this earth provided finance is available to explore these possibilities. But unfortunately finance becomes available only at a certain rate of interest. Projects which do not assure the going rate of interest to the financier starve for funds. Millions of human beings are unemployed only because the money-lender insists on his pound of flesh. All programmes of human development, education, training, scientific research, and construction of infrastructure require finance which becomes available only at a cost.

The lesson of the 20th century appears to be that full employment is not possible until we can attain 'euthanasia of the rentier'. Therefore, the challenge of the 21st century lies in inventing a mechanism for providing finance on an interest-free basis. If man is able to discover such a mechanism he would be able to unshackle himself from the bonds of money. It would usher in an era of human supremacy over money rather than money over human beings. Although interest on finance has been denounced by all religions and thinkers of various shades of thought throughout the ages, very little serious effort has been made to find out a practicable mechanism to provide institutional finance on an interest-free basis. The 21st century should accept the challenge of liberating man from the bonds of finance.

In many ways, the stage is set for such an endeavour. On the economic front, the debt trap, stagflation, unemployment, and growing disparity between the rich and the poor nations are some of the compulsions posed by the 20th century. The awareness of the atrocities of interest is increasing and the need for interest-free finance is being felt. On the political front, the dramatic changes in the communist countries and the long-range fears of internal contradictions leading to some identical blow-up in the capitalist world, compel us to evolve an un-exploitative framework so that the 21st century would become the century of hope for man.

There has been an increasing realization in the UN and various regional organizations to give greater importance to the development of man. But these programmes miss the essential point. Man shall never be able to develop if he remains subservient to finance. He must release himself from its clutches. The availability of interest-free finance would enable man to harness vast areas of land. It would eradicate unemployment and under-employment to an extent that could obliterate fiscal deficit and help in calling a halt to inflation. On the international front, the present outflow of resources from the poor to the rich nations in the form of interest would stop. The poor nations would toil for their own betterment and not for the betterment of their money-lenders. It would be, in Keynes' words, a 'sea-change' for humanity.

We should enter the 21st century with the resolve to develop a practical mechanism to make finance available free of cost. All other strategies to promote world prosperity and peace are likely to fail if adequate finance is not available. Therefore, we should try to overcome the most insurmountable of all obstacles first. It would lead to an era of prosperity for all.

The suggestion seems to be utopian. But history gives us hope and courage. There was a time when ideas like abolition of slavery, the introduction of adult suffrage, education-for-all, and equality between men and women were wild dreams of visionaries. A few decades back, let alone a few centuries, all these ideas were considered as impractical as is the vision of an interest-free world today. Given the ingenuity and will of man, however, this dream can also come true. It would make the 21st century worth living. It would virtually transform the whole earth into a heaven.

The present book aims at showing the contours of an Islamic economy. Its main theme is that the neo-classical economics which has fashioned the present-day world has outlived its utility. Its approach is narrow, its assumptions are unrealistic, and its strategies inhuman. It has landed humanity into an abyss of problems. If human thinking does not transcend the basic framework of neo-classical economics, the future of man on this globe is pretty bleak.

In this background, the Islamic economic precepts provide a ray of hope. The present book invites the reader to cast an objective look at the principles of Islamic economics and perceive their potential. The book addresses both the common reader and the professional economist trained in the West. It is not, however, a detailed exposition of the subject. Instead, it attempts to give a bare introduction to the subject of Islamic economics.

Chapter one gives a broad overview of the subject. It is intended for those who cannot spare the time to go through the entire book. It is a quick run-through of the main themes of the subject.

Chapters two and three are more in the nature of an academic excursion into formalizing the basic precepts of Islamic economics. They define the subject and spell out its scope and methodology. They are meant for professional economists and students of Islamic economics at the university level.

Chapter four gives a brief resume of the practice of Islamic economics in the present day world. It shows the eagerness of the Muslim countries to put into practice, albeit inadequately, the basic principles of Islamic economics.

The last two chapters argue that Islamic economics is the economics of the future and that neo-classical economics can benefit from its principles and methodology.

Two appendices follow the main text. The first discusses the liability of the shareholders in a joint stock company. The second deals with discounting for project evaluation. We believe that as compared to capitalism, Islam has a distinctive position on these issues. But the main text could not afford their discussion as it would have disturbed the balance and continuity of the book. Therefore, we have made them into appendices. We have added a select bibliography of recent writings on Islamic economics to help a serious reader pursue the subject further. We believe that the book will be able to stimulate further thinking toward establishing an interest-free world economy imbued with the Islamic values and norms of behaviour. We fervently hope that the prejudice of the modern world against religion will not undermine the rationality and objectivity of the contemporary man. We hope that the people of our age, who are likely to close the present century in a state of despair, will see a ray of hope in the principles of the Islamic economic order.

February 28, 1993. Muhammad Akram Khan

ACKNOWLEDGEMENT

I bow my head before Allah Almighty who enabled me to write this book. I have benefited from the writings of numerous scholars. I am unable to mention their names. But I owe a special debt to Dr. Zafar Ishaq Ansari, who not only persuaded me to finalize this work but also took great pains to improve it. I have no word to thank him for the hard work he did to revise the manuscript. I am also indebted to an anonymous referee who pointed out a large number of weaknesses in an earlier version of this book. But for the great help of these scholars this book would not have been in its present shape. May Allah accept their efforts and reward them. I alone am responsible for remaining weakness of this work.

Muhammad Akram Khan

ONE

ISLAMIC ECONOMICS: AN OVERVIEW

The main objective of the present book is to present an outline of the general framework of Islamic economics with a view to showing its relevance for the present-day economic order. The contemporary economic systems have failed to solve the economic problems of mankind and the Islamic economic order presents a ray of hope for the redemption of humanity from the quagmire of economic problems. The defeat of socialism is too obvious to be documented after what has happened in Eastern Europe and USSR during the last few years. The track record of capitalism is also not very promising. Although a small minority has achieved unprecedented high material standards of living, yet a vast majority of the people on the globe is still living under conditions of abject poverty. Even in the industrially advanced countries the problems of unemployment, inflation, poverty amidst affluence, unequal distribution of wealth, frequent bouts of business recessions, environmental pollution and ecological imbalance, to name a few, still bedevil man's present life and threaten his future. We need not mention that the focus of prosperity of these countries is uni-directional. It concentrates on the material dimension of life and completely ignores its spiritual, ethical, and social dimensions.

With the retreat of socialism, the erstwhile socialist countries are eagerly looking forward to adopt market capitalism — the system which they rejected about half a century ago. So impatient are they to enbrace acpitalism that they have hardly paused for a moment to think whether they will be able to establish an exploitation-free human economic order in the search of which they have rejected socialism. In all probability, these countries will soon become markets for the industrially advanced Western Europe, US and Japan. In fact, their markets have already flooded with the products of the capitalist countries. They are keen to imitate the lifestyles of the rich capitalist countries for which they will have to adopt the same economic strategies as the industrially advanced countries had followed. The results would be no different.

In pursuit of a materially abundant lifestyle they will end up with a similarly distorted prosperity. The financial institutions of the capitalist world are already spreading their network to these countries and in a few years the people of these countries would also be trapped in interest-bearing finance. They would toil hard to repay the loans and interest on these loans to the financial institutions of the rich countries. The day is not far when it would dawn upon the erstwhile socialist countries that they are no happier in their newly-won freedom from socialism.

It is our contention that there is an economic order other than the capitalist and socialist economic orders which has the potential of ushering in an age of human bliss. This economic order has been presented by Islam. Islam casts a comprehensive look at the human economic problems. It promises a free, just and responsible world for everyone on this earth. It treats all human beings in a similar manner and rejects the monopoly of a few nations on the resources of the earth.

The present chapter proposes to discuss the basic assumptions of Islamic economics. It will, then, take up the questions of economic organization, the role of money, consumer behaviour, the problem of poverty, fiscal management, research and development and the strategy for change. Obviously, such a vast field cannot be covered comprehensively in a short chapter purporting to give an overview. Therefore, we shall content ourselves with making short remarks to present a total picture. Each component of the picture would require a similar chapter for a detailed treatment which is out of the scope of the present book. (For useful discussion of the subject see M. U. Chapra, *Islam and the Economic Challenge*, Leicester: The Islamic Foundation and The International Institute of Islamic Thought, 1992). Since the Islamic economic order has some outward similarities with capitalism, such as the recognition of private property, free market, social security system, etc., we shall try to delineate the difference between Islam and capitalism in each major area.

1. ISLAMIC WORLDVIEW

God, according to the Islamic view, has created the universe for the benefit of all human beings. God has made the resources of this earth available to man who has the responsibility to make use of them, to mould them, and transform them according to his needs. God has given man the necessary apparatus to cultivate his faculties, to understand himself and nature, and to develop the means to nourish himself and satisfy his needs. But man is supposed to observe certain limits in the exercise of his freedom. Within these bounds all his acts are worship of God. Nothing remains profane or secular. This belief fills man with an enthusiasm to proceed continually in his pursuit to discover, understand, live and enjoy this world without having any feeling of guilt, — provided he seeks to please God and lives within the limits prescribed by Him — that such acts constitute indulgence in profanity or sin.[1]

Islam requires man to maintain a balance between his love for and abstinence from material things.[2] This counsel of restraint in the acquisition of material resources is true for the entire humanity. The requirement is that man should not cause the non-renewable resources of the earth to be recklessly depleted.[3] Every generation should show consideration for the future generations in the use of resources.[4] At the global level all nations should exercise restraint in the use of the resources of the earth.

Islām treats all human beings as children of Adam.[5] As human beings they are all equal.[6] It visualizes equal opportunities for everyone. It opposes the creation of monopolies. It liberates man from the bonds of other human beings. It envisages a society where everyone is self-reliant. At the global scale, it expects all nations of the world to live a respectable life. Thus the present-day situation in which the poor countries are heavily indebted to the rich countries is not in conformity with the Islamic vision of the world. By the same token, according to the Islamic vision, justice should be provided to everyone and to all nations. It is opposed to all forms of exploitation. Islam encourages a free market economy but with a degree of government intervention that would prevent the building up of concentration of economic power.

As the vicegerent of God man is accountable to Him for all his actions on the Day of Judgment. Thus Islam prescribes a strong system of accountability at all levels. This is true at the international level as well. The present situation in which certain powerful nations and global corporations are not accountable to anyone in this world is not in consonance with the Islamic Worldview. Islam envisages a world in which everyone with authority is accountable for his actions. It aims at the establishment of an economic order in which all nations of the world would get together to devise a global arrangement to monitor and check irresponsible behaviour by any nation. The resources of the earth must be safeguarded against waste,[7] reckless depletion, and destruction for narrow economic gains.

2. BASIC ASSUMPTIONS

2.1 Human Nature

Conventional economic analysis assumes that human beings are inherently selfish, that their primary concern is to derive maximum satisfaction or utility; and that in so doing they maximize the utility of the society as a whole. As a result, under capitalism the selfish behaviour of individuals and nations is not only rationalized but also encouraged. At the individual level, a starkly selfish and individualistic attitude which shows little concern for the betterment of others is accepted as reasonable. At the national plane, it is considered perfectly legitimate both for individuals and nations to adopt policies which serve selfish interests. This assumption has been widely criticized in the light of everyday observation and the findings of other social sciences such as psychology, sociology, and anthropology.

Islam, however, recognizes the dual nature of human beings. Human beings are selfish as well as altruistic. It does not, however, encourage human selfishness. Instead, it seeks to control human selfishness. It channelizes the selfishness of people to common good and prevents men from hurting others. It energizes their altruistic motives and arouses them to help one another. Consequently, the Islamic economic order visualizes a third sector, besides the private and public sectors, known as the voluntary sector. It recognizes that every individual, besides serving his selfish interests, should play a positive role in promoting common good by helping other human beings. Thus, it propagates that everyone can and should make a contribution to creating a better society.

2.2 Materialism

The capitalist economic order places a very high value on material attainments. In fact, progress and material possessions are used synonymously. The capitalist approach to life has resulted in widespread depletion of non-renewable natural resources, deforestation of wide areas, pollution of environment, and ecological imbalance.[8]

Islam treats material possessions as embellishments of life. But it treats them as secondary to the moral and spiritual development of human personality.[9] It does encourage enterprise and effort to increase one's material well-being, but it also enjoins that the focus of human striving on this earth is to obey God and to achieve His pleasure in the Hereafter. This change in the focus of human striving introduces a balanced approach to economic development. The Islamic approach visualizes a restraint in the human endeavour to increase material consumption. It supplements material accomplishments with the moral and spiritual growth of personality as desired goals.

2.3 Ownership

Capitalism visualizes an absolute right to private ownership so far as it is not acquired by damaging another person's similar right. Consequently, people are free to make use of their resources the way they like. For example, if they so choose, they may destroy and squander some of their resources. They are free to consume, save, invest (or lend on interest) whatever they own. They have an unlimited freedom to engage in any activity or profession. They can invest their money in any trade or occupation, even if it is socially harmful or destructive.

Islam recognizes the right of absolute ownership for God only. Man has been granted the right to benefit from the resources of the earth. He can earn his livelihood through lawful (*ḥalāl*) means. He is not totally free to consume, save or invest his earnings in any way he likes. There are definite moral limits on his right to earn, consume, save and invest. Within this general framework, Islam accepts the right of a person to sell, bequeath and leave for his heirs the property which he happens to own. Thus the Islamic concept of property limits human freedom to the use of the resources of the earth. It holds everyone accountable to God for the proper use of those resources.

2.4 Universalism

Capitalist economics has not been able to come out of the general framework conceived by its founding fathers in the eighteenth century. The time when *The Wealth of Nations* was written by Adam Smith (d.1776), most of the present-day rich countries were pursuing their colonial goals. The ideas of Adam Smith rationalized the notion of the nation-state. *The Wealth of Nations* provided a philosophical basis for a narrow approach to global economic issues. Instead of conceiving the world as a place for all human beings, it rationalized the concept of national policies in isolation from other peoples of the world. It introduced a chauvinistic approach towards economic problems, giving the industrially advanced countries an unbridled right to pursue whatever policies suited them. The same approach still persists. Individual states take economic decisions in their selfish interest. This is not to deny the fact that they do study the situation around them. However, they continue to adopt policies which suit their selfish ends ignoring the effects such policies might have on other nations. In this process, the people of the whole world suffer.[10]

The Islamic view is that the entire world has been created by God for the benefit of all human beings. There is, thus, a great need for all the peoples of the world to consult and cooperate with one another while pursuing economic policies which might adversely affect others. Although lip service is being paid to the need for greater international cooperation, in practice human beings have not made any significant progress in that direction. It is time for people to transcend the conventional economic ideas and build a global economy on the basis of equality and mutual cooperation.

3. ECONOMIC ORGANIZATION

3.1 Economic Power

To put it very succinctly, the present-day capitalist economies are organized on the basis of free market mechanism where production of goods and services comes from a combination of capital and wage labour. The capital is provided both as equity and as interest-bearing loan. The market, though theoretically free, is dominated by mega-corporations which determine the price level and thus influence the level of investment, saving, production, and consumption.[11] The classical economic analysis which was based on the immutable law of perfect competition has become irrelevant due to the concentration of economic power in the hands of mega-corporations.

The accumulation of economic power in the capitalist economies is caused by a number of factors. First, the interest income of the rentier class turns the flow of wealth from the poor to the rich, which gradually enables a small minority to accumulate large amounts of wealth.[12] Second, the legal innovations of incorporation and limited liability have enabled the corporations to collect huge amounts of capital on account of limited risk.[13] While the entitlement of the shareholders of a corporation to the profits is unlimited, the risk to bear the loss is limited to the extent of their own capital.[14] Third, the benefits of technological developments are not passed on to the consumers in the form of lower prices which would benefit the labourers as well. Instead, the gains from technological development are mainly appropriated by the mega - corporations which enjoy near monopolistic power to fix prices.

3.2 Equilibrium at Less than Full Employment

Another feature of the capitalist economies is that they can be at equilibrium without attaining the full employment level. This question has been widely discussed in Keynesian economics. The main reason for this is the existence of interest on capital. It subdues investment and, through it, effective demand. Consequently, the market mechanism, by itself, is unable to achieve full employment. It requires active public policy to encourage investment. At the same time, the private sector feels the compulsion of promoting the sale of their goods and services so that the return on their investment is assured. As a result, the economy has to create demand artificially by resorting to ruthless campaigns of advertisements on television and the news media. The consumers are hooked, day in and day out, to the temptation of buying more and more goods and services. The capitalist system is forced to create demand artificially so as to keep the system going.

The above is indeed a sketchy picture of the economic organization under contemporary capitalism. To do full justice to the subject a much more detailed account would be required. However, these hints should suffice to indicate the difference between the pattern of economic organization of Islam and capitalism.

3.3 Islamic Economic Organization

Islam prescribes a free market based on supply and demand. At the same time, it ensures that the economic power is not accumulated and if it does, it is diluted in the following manner:

(a) Islam has prohibited interest on capital and thus has foreclosed the door of accumulating wealth without work or without assuming risk.[15] The general rule is that whoever wants to earn a profit must assume risk as well.[16] The operating principle is : no risk, no gain.

(b) Islam visualizes a society where an individual is not dependent on others. It recognizes the need of each individual to actualize his potential abilities. Thus, it visualizes a society where a maximum number of people are independent in their earning and living. This is also one of the implications of belief in One God who is the sustainer of the entire universe. The Messenger of God (peace be upon him) indicated his preference for this pattern of livelihood when he raised the status of slaves to that of brothers and partners.[17] Traditionally, the Muslim societies have placed a low value on wage-labour. Instead, they have always encouraged self-employment or such forms of business as *shirkaḥ* or *mudārabah*.[18] It was the capitalist mode of production which, for the first time in human history, made large chunks of population dependent on capitalists for their livelihood.[19] The Islamic economy would encourage such forms of business where people would join hands, preferably in the form of partners, and not as employees and workers. Once this principle is accepted, the details of the socio-economic relationships can be worked out. But one thing is obvious. Such an economic organization spreads the ownership base over the whole economy and forestalls the accumulation of economic power.

(c) Islamic ethos does not encourage unplanned introduction of new technology. On the one hand, it would require that the introduction of technology should be phased and planned.[20] Moreover, it would urge the industrialists to bear the cost of the dislocation or economic hardship created by the introduction of new technology. The basis for such public policies is the general principle that cost and benefit go hand in hand.[21] One who earns a profit must pay for the cost as well. Moreover, once the economy is organized on the principle of worker ownership, the benefits of new technology would automatically spread over to the whole economy.

(d) Since Islamic economy does not allow interest on loan capital, in all probability interest-free business credit will not be available on a large scale. Consequently, the question of limited liability of the shareholders in a joint stock company would lose much of its relevance. In this manner Islamic economy would shut off another channel for accumulating the economic power. (For a discussion of the point see Appendix-I)

(e) The Islamic economy discourages such market malpractices as hoarding with a view to raising prices (*iḥtikār*), collusion to bid up prices (*tanājush*), counter-bidding (*tasāwum*), efforts to forestall genuine competition by discouraging the sellers to reach the market (*bay' talaqqī al-rukbān*), and middlemanship by shrewd people to deprive the sellers of the best price available (*bay' al-hāḍir li bād*). These were typical practices in the market to weaken genuine competition in the days of the Prophet (peace be upon him). On this analogy, one may claim that all market practices which lead to monopolies or which weaken the forces of competition should be discouraged to-day in an Islamic economy. One thing is almost certain. The present-day Islamic economy will have to develop some new channels of market information for keeping the buyers and sellers informed of the market situation. This information will have to be cheap and easily available. Availability of relevant and timely information will discourage cheating, fraud, collusion, and exploitation of others on account of their ignorance.

(f) In an Islamic economic order the problem of demand creation through advertisement would also not remain as serious as we find it in a capitalist dispensation. In the absence of interest, the brakes on the expansion of investment will be removed. The economy is likely to settle at full employment or near full employment level. The business organizations will have a lesser compulsion to create demand artificially through advertisements. The extent, coverage, purpose and cost of advertisements in the Islamic economy will also undergo a change. But this question does not concern us at the moment. The question as to how the Islamic economy would keep itself going, where demand creation would not be a normal practice, needs some consideration. As we have discussed, Islam seems to prefer a society where the ownership of resources is widely dispersed. Islam would also like to maintain a high level of effective demand so that the resources remain fully employed. To achieve that end the Islamic economy has a mechanism of transferring wealth from the rich to the poor. It has made obligatory on everyone who owns a certain minimum of wealth to pay a fixed sum as *zakāh* for expenditure on the welfare of the poor and the needy. Besides, it encourages *infāq* which signifies voluntary spending on one's relations and neighbours and on other social needs. The Islamic law of inheritance also contributes to the dispersion of wealth on a wide scale. Thus Islam visualizes transfer of sufficient purchasing power to the poor to keep the effective demand high enough for achieving a full employment equilibrium.

4. ROLE OF MONEY

4.1 Interest and Public Debt

In the capitalist world money is treated as a commodity besides being a medium of exchange and measure of value. Like other commodities, it has a price. One has to pay its price if one wants to borrow it. This price is termed as interest. There is ample evidence since ancient times to show that interest is a powerful instrument for perpetration of injustice. In the present age the tyranny of interest has become manifest in the form of the huge public debts of the developing countries. Over the years the public debts of low income economies had accumulated to over $ 426 billion by 1991.[22] Since 1982 the amount of aid flowing into the developing countries has been less than the amount being paid out by those countries in the form of interest and principal.[23] The debt servicing includes more than 50% interest and year after year the amount of interest is growing.[24] This means that there is a net resource outflow from the poor countries to the rich countries. The poor countries are toiling hard just to pay their earnings to the rich rentier nations.

4.2 Interest and Foreign Exchange Instability

Interest differentials play a vital role in the volatility of foreign exchange markets. The financial markets of the world shift about 200 billions dollars from one place to another every day. Ninety per cent of these movements of foreign exchange are speculative and merely seek to earn differential in the rates of interest and exchange rate.[25] These transactions remain active almost round the clock. These fund transfers lead to fluctuations in the exchange rates which reinforce the tendency to shift funds. Interest on capital is a major factor in the instability of the international monetary system.

4.3 Interest and Environment

Interest plays an important role in vitiating and polluting the environment. The developing countries overuse their soil, thus turning good land to desert since they are under immense pressure to repay their debts with interest.[26] The developing countries, being faced with huge debts and balance of payments difficulties, turn to such institutions as IMF and World Bank. The conditionalities imposed by these institutions force the developing countries to increase their exports for which they are compelled to mine their environmental resources more deeply.[27]

4.4 Interest and Inflation

The adverse effects of interest on employment and its role in causing business cycles are well known. However, uptil now the conventional economics had believed that interest and inflation had an inverse relationship. As a result, public policies had pleaded for raising of interest rate to combat inflation. But recent research has shown that inflation and interest are directly correlated.[28] This is so because interest enters into the cost of production and the corporations recover it through increased price of the output. The corporations can shift the burden of interest on to the customers because of the economic power they enjoy in fixing the price level. At the state level, the governments tend to live beyond their means. They borrow huge sums in the name of 'development'. But they are unable to generate enough resources to repay the principal and interest thereon. This leads to deficit financing, which fans the fire of inflation with the result that to-day the whole world is in the grip of inflation but no one has the courage to identify the real culprit — interest on capital.

4.5 Islamic Concept of Money

As compared to capitalism, Islam treats money as a medium of exchange and a store of value but not as a commodity, since money by itself cannot perform any function. It becomes useful only when it is exchanged into a real asset or when it is used to buy a service. Therefore, it cannot be sold or bought on credit. One needs to appreciate the great wisdom of the Prophet (peace be upon him) who, guided by revelation, not only declared interest on loan as unlawful but also banned exchange of money and some other valuables for an unequal quantity and on deferred payment basis if the commodity or currency was the same.[29] The net effect of this was to prevent interest from penetrating into the economic system through the back door. Thus the economic order of Islam, by prohibiting interest, takes care of the problems of unemployment, inflation, foreign exchange volatility, business cycles, and excessive depletion of natural resources

4.6 Banking in Islamic Economy

The banking system in an Islamic economy is based on the concept of sharing profit as well as loss. The general principle is that those who want to earn a return on their savings should also be willing to assume a risk. The banks will have to share the loss of the enterprise as well if they wish to obtain a return on their capital.

The importance of equity capital in economic development is now well appreciated in the financial circles. A truly Islamic financial structure would be one wherein like other factors of production capital is also required to bear risk. Once interest-based transactions are abolished from the banking system and capital is available on equity basis, the volatile transfers of capital will also subside. The world financial wizards will no longer be keen to lend their money to the enviable Third World countries. The Third World countries which have incurred large debts have not always borrowed out of their genuine needs. Instead, quite often the financial institutions of the rich countries, which found themselves with a liquidity glut (especially after the 1973 oil crisis), found a profitable channel of investment for their surplus funds in the poor countries and somehow managed to inundate them with loans. The financial institutions set up their 'development' departments to hook more clients. These institutions provided their clients with consultancy services, often on a *gratis* basis, and did most of the paper work on their behalf and identified attractive projects for them.[30] Thus the demand for interest-bearing loans was created by the banks themselves. If in a system like the one visualized by Islam, the lure of interest is removed and banks are made to share the loss on investment as they have a share of the returns, the size of public debt will also shrink. In fact, the global debt will remain only to the extent of trade credits of a routine nature. Consequently, the present outflow of resources from the poor countries to the rich countries will also stop and the world will be a much happier place to live in.

5. CONSUMER BEHAVIOUR

5.1 Consumerism

The consumer behaviour in the capitalist economies is explained in terms of the sovereignty of consumers. It is contended that one is free to buy anything one likes. There are no moral checks on that.

But the consumers are excessively influenced by the onslaught of advertisements. The temptation to buy new things is promoted as a social value which rates the pursuit of novelty very high. Psychologically, the consumers are persuaded to feel proud of themselves if they are in possession of something novel as compared to others in their social circle. Such a value system tends to stigmatize as inferior all who fail to acquire the new things possessed by their peers and neighbours. This creates an impulse to catch up and beat others leading to a never-ceasing rat race. The rich economies of the capitalist countries have become mass consumption societies with a great deal of waste.[31]

The effect of such an attitude is that the people living in developed countries, who are barely 25 per cent of the globe's population, consume 15 times as much paper, 10 times as much steel, and 12 times as much energy as the rest of the 75 per cent people of the world.[32] It is obvious that the resources of the world are just not sufficient to afford the same lifestyle for everyone on this earth. There is a great need for restraint. But the capitalist system does not have a mechanism to restrain people from wasteful consumption. Instead, its banks, media, business corporations, and governments all have a vested interest in encouraging consumption so that a high level of investment is sustained. Instead of abolishing interest which would remove the brakes from the free flow of capital to productive channels, a topsy turvy approach of increasing consumption is adopted in order to keep the wheels of the economy moving.

5.2 Simple Living and Intensive Use of Resources

The kind of economy that seems to harmonize with the Islamic ethos is a low consumption economy. The Islamic approach would require individuals to use the resources as intensively as possible and not to replace them until they have truly outlived their utility. The Prophet (peace be upon him) placed a very high premium on simple living and discouraged people from luxuries. This is not to suggest that Islam would like people to live a life of deprivation and misery even when they are in a position to afford a higher standard of living. Islam visualizes an egalitarian society where relative differences in socio-economic conditions will be a lot less than what we observe in the capitalist societies. The Islamic view of life would require that those who can afford to have a higher material standard should voluntarily forego some of their comforts and help others improve their economic lot so as to enjoy a similar life-style. It is only after most of the people have acquired a comparable living standard that the society as a whole should move to a higher socio-economic level.[33]

5.3 Islamic Values and Consumer Behaviour

The value system of Islam supports the above consumption pattern. In an Islamic society *taqwā* (God-consciousness) is considered very highly. The more a person is God-conscious, the more highly he is esteemed in the society. *Taqwā* comprises a cluster of values like justice (*'adl*), benevolence (*iḥsān*), benevolent spending in the cause of God (*infāq*), remembering God (*dhikr*), etc. *Taqwā* is a multi-dimensional value. One can excel in it by cultivating a number of virtues in oneself. People who seek a good status in an Islamic society try to excel in *taqwā*. In the economic jargon we may say that *taqwā* is a 'satiable comfort'. It diverts the energies of the people away from acquisitiveness to a sustained effort aimed at spiritual self-enrichment and social improvement.

5.4 Conservation of Resources

Islam visualizes an economy where the resources are conserved rather than depleted and consumed away.[34] In the context of the present time, the Islamic approach would require a close cooperation among all the countries of the world to conserve non-renewable resources of the earth. In order to enforce discipline it would prescribe a system of monitoring and evaluation of the policies of individual countries relating to use of the non-renewable resources. It would also recommend an environmental audit of individual countries by an international board of auditors. This would require an international mechanism of accountability to enforce environment-safe policies.

6. POVERTY

6.1 Contemporary Economic Order

The people of the world who are poor today are larger in number than they were a decade ago.[35] The difference between the poor and the rich countries of the world is increasing.[36] The conventional economic theories, the most prominent being the 'trickle down effect', have failed to alleviate poverty in the world.[37] Instead, the present economic order has led to a transfer of resources from the poor to the rich countries. The policies of the rich countries to subsidize their own farmers, the trade barriers placed by them against the commodities of the poor countries, the efforts of the poor countries to increase their commodity output out of their anxiety to generate foreign exchange to repay debts, are some of the factors which pushed the commodity prices downward during the eighties.[38] As a result, the per capita growth rates of some of the poorest countries have even been negative during this period.

6.2 Social and Political Underdevelopment

Despite this, it cannot be denied that a number of countries have made serious efforts to build the economic infrastructure necessary for development. But the essential question remains as to why these efforts have not been able to achieve a breakthrough. The reasons seem to be primarily more social and political rather than economic.

(a) The roots of this underdevelopment are deeply imbedded in the philosophy of development which these countries have pursued. Development, according to the prevalent theories, means increase in the physical stock of capital and infrastructure. The celebrated GNP has been the focus of all development effort regardless of the consideration how it is increased and who benefits from such an increase. In the process the Third World countries have badly ignored their own people. They have paid inadequate attention to the productive capacities of their people.

(b) While concerted effort has been made to create and increase the physical capital, the worth of the human capital has scarcely been fully appreciated. The affairs of these countries are handled by bureaucrats and politicians without involving the ordinary people of those countries. They do not have access to public organizations nor do they enjoy the protection of law. They have been marginalised with the result that they have very little incentive to undertake the effort required to improve their lot.

(c) The poor people of these countries do not have access to the resources of their country. The number of landless labourers is very high. Even those who happen to have a piece of land do not have access to finance, technology, water supply, market, fertilizer and pesticides. Therefore, they soon sell off this land and prefer to become labourers again.

(d) There is rampant corruption in all the Third World countries. Corrupt military and civil bureaucracies rule these countries. Corruption is employed to keep the people deprived of resources. A favourite class is groomed by means of licenses, permits, and cheaper foreign exchange, etc. In this process, majority of the people are marginalised.[39]

6.3 Over-population

The whole problem of underdevelopment is often summarized in a wolf-cry against population explosion. The fact is that the slogan of 'over-population' is a hoax. The cases of South Korea and Taiwan may. be compared with those of Bangladesh and India. The per person cultivated area in Bangladesh is 0.23 acres and in India it is 0.45 acres. But the per person cultivated area in South Korea and Taiwan is 0.12 and 0.13 acres respectively. Yet the two formerly mentioned countries are treated as over-populated. The reason is that the output per acre in the former countries is much smaller than the output in the latter countries. The technology to improve the output is available but the farmers do not have access to it.[40]

The governments of the poor countries have not realized that the potential of human beings to improve things is immense. The greatest asset of a nation are its people provided they have the opportunities to develop their potentialities. And this requires that the public policies should seek to:

- provide the poor with access to resources;
- involve the poor in decision-making at the local level;
- provide protection to the poor against the economically powerful minority; and
- encourage as well as enforce honesty in public administration.

6.4 Urbanization

Another tragedy of the poor countries is unbalanced Urbanization. Socio-economic development in these countries has been so planned that resources flow continuously from the rural to the urban areas. The physical facilities of education, water supply, sewerage, telecommunication and health care are concentrated in the urban centres. As a result, there is a continuous influx of population towards the cities. The size of the cities is increasing, adding more slums and putting an increasing pressure on civic services.

6.5 Technology

Unplanned introduction of new technology is another sore point in the development effort of these countries. With each new breakthrough in technological development, a number of people lose their livelihood and need rehabilitation. But there is no systematic arrangement to retrain or rehabilitate those who lose their jobs as a result of new technology.

6.6 Social Security System

The social security services are often inadequate in the developing countries because of resource constraints. But the efforts made in this direction remain ineffective because of bureaucratic inefficiency, mismanagement, corruption, and the problem of 'free rider'. The local people are not drawn into the administration of these social services. The accountability apparatus is either missing or too weak. Consequently, these efforts have not been able to make any dent in the problem of poverty.

6.7 Fighting Poverty in an Islamic Framework

Poverty is a complex phenomenon. Islamic scholars are developing a body of doctrines to analyze and solve this problem. Some of the ideas circulated so far are:

(a) An Islamic strategy to fight poverty should have its distinct orientation in so far as the development effort is focused on human beings. It concentrates on the development of productive capacities of the people by education and skill training.[41]

(b) The people ought to be organized in local cooperatives and made incharge of their own affairs.[42] They should take all the decisions relating to themselves. This would give them an incentive for self-development and would involve them in the overall development effort.

(c) Finance should be made available through cooperative banks on profit-loss sharing basis. People should be provided access to physical resources and to public organizations by encouraging them to organize themselves locally.

(d) Islam has laid great stress on honest government. Perhaps, it was for the first time in human history, that Islam introduced the distinction between private property and public property and made the rulers accountable to the people. In the present age, an Islamic society should strengthen its system of accountability in a similar manner. A number of new institutions will have to be established for this purpose.

(e) The Islamic strategy of development should focus on human needs. It should begin by making an assessment of human needs in terms of health, education, clean water, clean air, telecommunication and transport and then translate it into the investment required to fulfil these needs.

(f) Since Islam lays great stress on the self-reliance and independence of human beings, the Islamic strategy for development should not visualize borrowing from other countries on interest, even as an *ad hoc* measure. However, it should encourage cooperation between different countries on the basis of equity participation in joint ventures or in the form of grants or interest-free loans.

(g) As a short-term measure, Islamic economics would recommend that as a way out of the present indebtedness the rentier nations should write off interest on their outstanding loans and convert the outstanding amounts — the principal — into equity capital of various public enterprises of the debtor countries. This will reduce the burden of the poor countries and will also reduce the outflow of resources from the poor to the rich countries.

(h) Islam does not treat human beings as a liability. Instead, they are the most precious asset of any country.[43] Therefore, an Islamic development strategy should be geared to develop the potentialities of the people by education and skill training and remove obstacles in their way to having access to resources of the economy.

(i) The Islamic concept of economic justice revolts against the prevalent strategy of unbalanced development between rural and urban areas. As human beings, people in the villages are equally entitled to receive basic facilities such as education, health, transport, drinking water, electricity and telecommunication. The conventional investment criteria which uses cost-benefit analysis to determine the suitability of investment will undergo a change if investment is done with a view to developing human beings wherever they may live. As a first priority, an Islamic government in the present age will have to adopt the policies that will bridge the existing gap between the rural and urban areas and provide a similar lifestyle to all.

(j) Islamic economics visualizes a planned introduction of technology. As a practical measure, an Islamic state in the present age can institute a fund to which contributions may be made by the entrepreneurs out of the super-profits they earn by introducing new technologies. This fund will be used to re-train and rehabilitate those who lose their jobs as a result of the introduction of new technology.

(k) On top of all these measures, the Islamic system of *zakāh* would provide social security at the local level. The people of a locality should so organize their affairs that they may collect a prescribed percentage of their wealth to maintain and rehabilitate those who cannot meet both their ends meet. Since the collection and distribution of *zakāh* is required to be done locally, the problem of 'free rider' is also taken care of to a large extent. It is far more difficult for a person to remain on dole when the transfer grants are being given by the local people than when they are administered centrally by an anonymous state bureaucracy.[44] In an Islamic set-up social security is, primarily, the responsibility of the family. In case a person is not able to receive support from the family, the local community is required to look after such a person. Assistance from the central treasury of the state comes only when all the local arrangements fall short of resources.

7. FISCAL MANAGEMENT

7.1 Islamic Principles of Taxation

The Islamic principles of fiscal management are also distinct:

(a) The principal tax of *zakāh* which sets the trend for other taxation is simple to administer. Its rates are low. Its coverage is wide. Its incidence is in proportion to one's wealth so that people with greater means pay more than people with smaller means.

(b) *Zakāh* is collected locally by the people on behalf of the central government and distributed in the same locality. This principle takes care of a host of problems which arise due to regional complaints against transfer of resources from one locality to the other.

7.2 Deficit Financing

(a) The Islamic teachings of moderation (*iqtiṣād*) apply to state budget as well. The Islamic approach to economics would seem to favour a balanced budget. The evils of deficit financing are too obvious to need any mention here. The problem of creating effective demand by government intervention does not remain relevant in the context of Islamic economy since it abolishes interest which is the main obstacle in achieving full employment. However, if people want the government to play an active role in economic life, they must pay for it in the form of higher taxes. Borrowing for development — and that too on interest — is altogether alien to Islamic principles. However, in the case of long-term projects whose benefits will be spread over several generations, the state may raise interest-free loans in the interest of inter-generational equity. To alleviate the hardship of unemployment, social security schemes may also be introduced.

Fiscal management in the capitalist economies is topsy turvy. It relies on deficit financing to stimulate the economy. The whole cycle starts like this. Interest has an inverse relationship with the marginal efficiency of capital. The higher the rate of interest, the lower will be the marginal efficiency of capital and the lower will be the level of investment, leading to an increase in unemployment.

Taxes are levied to pay for social security benefits. When the burden of taxes becomes unbearable, governments borrow from banks and private savers on interest, which in turn adds to the public expenditure in the form of debt servicing, leading to a greater deficit and starting the vicious circle all over again.

In an Islamic economy, instead of getting into this vicious circle, the evil can be nipped in the bud. Since interest on capital is abolished, it will be possible for full employment equilibrium to take place. To cope with the problem of involuntary unemployment or other hardship cases, there are the institutions of *zakāh* and *infāq*. But these institutions would operate at the local levels. The state budget would not be overburdened with public debt or additional taxes to provide for social security benefits.

8. DIFFUSION OF KNOWLEDGE

Islam places a great emphasis on spreading knowledge and sharing it with others. Historically, Muslims have served as the means for transmitting knowledge to people of all regions and races. In fact the roots of Western progress in science and technology can be traced back to Muslim teachers and scientists. But the Western approach to knowledge is chauvinistic. It has introduced the concept of patents and proprietary rights. As a result, the developing nations have to pay heavy sums of money as royalties to the industrially advanced countries. For example, in 1980, the latest year for which data are available, the developing countries paid $ 2 billion by way of royalties and fees to the industrial countries.[45]

The Islamic perception is that all knowledge should be shared freely.[46] For this, not only the end result of research should be shared but also the developing countries should be closely involved in creating new knowledge. Bright and intelligent persons from all parts of the world should be associated with a free and open mind in research projects and encouragement should be provided to help people develop appropriate technological solutions for themselves. They should be helped to do so rather than made to buy inappropriate solutions to those problems at exorbitant prices. International institutions in which all nations of the world should contribute financial and human resources to conduct research and disseminate its results need to be developed. This is essential if the Western nations sincerely want to create a world where all human beings participate as equals. The mystification of all useful knowledge should end and ways and means should be found to share new developments in the realm of knowledge. Such a strategy will lay the foundation for a genuinely cooperative and friendly world.

9. CONCLUDING REMARKS

We have briefly discussed above the main features of an Islamic economy. While doing so we have compared them with the features of the contemporary capitalist economic order. Islam seeks to build a totally new economic order. Its strategy to build such an economy is, however, evolutionary rather than revolutionary.

This is manifest from the way the Prophet (peace be upon him) proceeded to change the society in his own days. The Prophet (peace be upon him) did not abolish interest in a single day. He decreed its abolition only when the economic situation was ripe to sustain such a change. First, he prohibited *ribā al-faḍl* (interest on barter exchange) and this foreclosed the entry of *ribā* (interest) from the back-door. Simultaneously, he encouraged a simple lifestyle so that the demand for consumers' credit does not, ordinarily, arise. Subsequently, the revenues from *ghanīmah* (war booty) and *fay'* opened the door of general prosperity so that people found themselves in possession of excess of capital instead of being short of it. The demand for loan capital decreased. For business transactions, sole proprietorship, *shirkah* and *muḍārabah* visualized unlimited liability of the financiers in repayment of debts, a rule which discouraged demand for loan capital. Thus the demand for business (loan) capital was not very high. However, it still existed in the form of credit sales. But the society could meet this demand since there was a general state of prosperity because of a variety of reasons, including the flow of funds from the several items of revenues. Therefore, capital could not command a scarcity price or opportunity cost. Thus the stage was set for an economic change as a result of which interest on loan capital could be abolished by a legal decree. This the Prophet (peace be upon him) did on the day of the Last Pilgrimage (10 AH).

The lesson that we can learn from the life of the Prophet (peace be upon him) is that economic changes cannot be brought about just by means of legal enactments. Nor can they be brought about without involving other people of the world. In recent decades, the world has greatly shrunk owing to revolution in communication. An action in one part of the world has its repercussions in other parts as well. Therefore, no effective change can be brought about without the willing cooperation of other nations.

The world order that conforms to the ideals of Islam has the potential to solve most of the problems of the present-day world. It is time that the people of the world cast an objective look at what Islam has to offer.

Table 1. Capitalism and Islam

Capitalism	Islamic Economic System
Human beings are selfish	Human beings are selfish as well as altruistic
Materialism is the supreme value	Materialism should be controlled
Absolute private ownership	Private ownership within a moral framework
Nation-state context	Global economy context
Economic power for the minority through: - Interest - Limited liability - Wage-labour - Primogeniture - Market imperfections	Economic power widely diffused through: - Equity participation - Worker ownership - Law of inheritance - Free market flows

Demand creation through advertisement	Demand creation through *infāq*, equitable laws, and inheritance
Money as a commodity besides being medium of exchange and store of value	Money as a medium of exchange and store of value, but not a commodity
Consumerism a value	Simple living a value
Economic development based on physical and material growth	Economic development through human and spiritual growth
Urbanization	Rural-urban balance
Unplanned technology	Planned technology
State-run social security system through secular taxes	Social security through - Family - Community - State
Deficit financing — a way of life	Balanced budget — a way of life
Mystification and protection of knowledge	Diffusion and sharing of knowledge

TWO

THE NATURE OF ISLAMIC ECONOMICS

1. THE RECENT UPSURGE

Islamic economics is a nascent discipline. It has not yet attracted much attention of the economic profession although the recent past has witnessed a sporadic intellectual activity in some Muslim countries which promises to make Islamic economics an independent branch of knowledge. This is evident from the fact that at present at least 30 universities in Muslim countries are offering undergraduate and post-graduate courses in Islamic economics. Quite a few Ph.D. theses in Western universities have been written on various issues relating to Islamic economics. There are three international research institutions exclusively devoted to the development and dissemination of knowledge relating to Islamic economics. Three scholarly research journals publish material on Islamic economics. Besides, a number of journals on Islam, Middle East and economics publish articles on Islamic economics. Thanks to the papers published in these journals and the many books which have appeared during the last two decades, a respectable body of serious literature on Islamic economics has accumulated.[1] There now exists an International Association of Islamic Economics with its headquarters in Jeddah which has started publishing a journal of its own.

Islamic economics presents Islam's viewpoint on the human economic situation. Its roots are in the sacred Islamic texts which provide broad guidelines for the economic behaviour of human beings. But a significantly large portion of its literature is the result of the human endeavour to analyze and to seek solutions to the economic problems of man in the overall framework of Islam. Therefore, there is little that is sacrosanct about most of what Islamic economists say concerning human economic problems. Muslim scholars have been discussing economic issues of their respective times during the last fourteen centuries. Some of these discussions have been preserved by history. Thus Islamic economics has a rich heritage of Muslim thinking to draw upon although most of it may not be precisely applicable to our own times. But it gives a fertile field for further inquiry, opening gateways to a distinct epistemology, method of analysis and investigation.

The recent upsurge[2] of interest in Islamic economics, after about two centuries of sluggish intellectual activity among Muslims, owes its origin to a number of factors. First, there is a great dissatisfaction with the way in which the mainstream economics seeks to analyze and find solutions to the economic problems of the world. The present era which boasts of material prosperity has not been able to do much about some of the endemic problems of the world. Unemployment combined with inflation, and widespread poverty in developing countries, misery amidst affluence, regional disparities, environmental pollution, the dissipation of moral values under the onslaught of technological innovations, the overwhelming economic power of global corporations, the waste of precious resources through reckless consumerism, international exploitation in the name of economic 'aid' and iniquitous trade structures are too familiar to be elaborated upon. All this has created an urge to look for a fresh approach to human problems.

Second, as discussed in chapter one, the mainstream neoclassical economics has a narrow basis, and has unrealistic assumptions about human nature and behaviour. Economists have widely questioned its approach and conclusions by emphasizing the need to revise its very premises. As we shall see shortly, Islamic economics has the potential to answer the need to have a more realistic basis for economic analysis.

Third, during the colonial era capitalism adopted an insensitive approach to indigenous cultural values, social institutions and local technology of the colonized nations. It systematically tried to destroy the traditional societies in the colonies on the plea that the capitalist system was more efficient and productive.[3] History has shown the hollowness of such assertions. The colonies became poorer when the colonial powers left them than when they occupied them. This has alienated the elite of those countries from the capitalist way of thinking. Of course, some of them turned to certain muddled forms of socialism or capitalism. But from among them some have looked up to the pristine values of Islam and imbibed the desire to reincarnate their bygone glory. There is no denying the fact that there is a certain amount of romanticism in the thinking of several of these people. But the phenomenon seems to be one of the causes for a growing interest in Islamic economics.

Fourth, the international economic order that has emerged as a result of the prevalent economic thinking has institutionalized exploitation of the poor countries by the rich. The disparity between the two is on the increase despite all the lip service to justice and fairplay. The terms of trade have systematically turned against the primary producers. The global economic mechanism has been designed to perpetuate the hegemony of the industrially advanced countries. It is now being widely realized that such an economic arrangement carries its own seeds of destruction.[4] There is, thus, a felt need for a fresh look at this economic order. We shall argue later in chapter five that Islamic economics holds this promise.

The dramatic changes in Eastern Europe since 1989 and the break up of USSR have also expedited the search for a better economic doctrine. It is clear that socialism as an economic system that would procure justice and prosperity for mankind has been finally defeated and people in the socialist countries are looking up to capitalism as a saviour and anchor of the last resort. Their disillusionment with socialism has shown them an easy route which leads to the same capitalism which they had abandoned less than half a century ago. After the dust settles down, those very countries would be obliged to re-think their strategy to achieve a sustained development and a more just and civilized society. It will be at that juncture that they are likely to have a serious look at what Islam has to offer as an alternative to both capitalism and socialism. Islamic economics brings a fresh approach to the human economic problems. It has the potential of ushering in a just and more humane civilization.

The theoretical work in the field of Islamic economics, however, remains scanty for several reasons. First, the Muslims who should have pioneered the development of this subject have suffered from an intellectual trauma. It came with the political domination of the West which not only destroyed the Muslim educational institutions but also damaged the spirit of inquiry in the Muslim lands. This has prevented the Muslims from developing knowledge from their own perspective and to the extent that the West has done. Second, the problem of intellectual space has also contributed to this phenomenon. The West is fully dominant on all seats of learning, and on publication and distribution of most of the serious literature in all disciplines. It documents, classifies and disseminates information on various disciplines throughout the world. Whatever efforts have been made by the scholars in Islamic economics have not been adequately taken note of in the West. Moreover, the scholarly journals published from the West do not easily accept the work of Muslim economists mainly because there is a strong aversion against all academic writings with a religious orientation. Third, there does not exist much empirical data to test or falsify the postulates of Islamic economics. This has posed an insurmountable problem to the Muslim economists.[5] Fourth, most of the professional economists are simply not aware of what Muslim economists are so zealously pleading. A tiny minority of Western economists, which is attracted towards Islamic economics, holds a variety of opinions. Some consider the work of Islamic economists to consist of apologetics. They say that the scholars of Islamic economics are engaged in grossly adapting Islamic postulates to Western theories.[6] Still others doubt the possibility of the development of an economic system capable of accommodating the contemporary economic reality from a few simple precepts.[7] Fifth, some of the Muslims are also victims of a romantic confusion about Islamic economics. Impressed by the apparent size and complexity of the capitalist and socialist economic systems, they think that the Islamic economic system must be an amalgam of capitalism, socialism and a few metaphysical beliefs of Islam. Such simplistic notions about Islamic economics are also a source of considerable misunderstanding.

The present chapter seeks to dispel these doubts, fears and confusions. It is an attempt to define the nature, scope and subject-matter of Islamic economics. As would be argued later, Islamic economics is not a denial of contemporary reality, nor does it seek to stage an about-turn towards the conditions of the seventh century Arab society. It only visualizes a reorganization of the basic economic functions. Islam has not provided a strait-jacket of economic relationships and institutions. Perhaps Islam could not do so as it would have been a negation of its own claim for universality.

The scheme of the rest of the chapter is as follows: First, we shall discuss briefly the Islamic worldview and its position on such issues as human nature, the position of man on the earth, and the relationship of man with the resources of the earth. Then we shall introduce Islamic economics as a branch of knowledge by giving a tentative definition and explaining its key concepts. This would be followed by a brief mention of the sources of Islamic economics. This shall be followed by a discussion on the approach of Islamic economics and the place of the economic system in the life-scheme of Islam.

2. DEFINITION OF ISLAMIC ECONOMICS

Islamic economics has been variously defined by Muslim economists. Irrespective of the actual phrasing, all the definitions emphasize the comprehensive character of the subject, based on the universal moral values of Islam. In the following discussion, we have attempted a definition of Islamic economics which captures the gist of the subject as discernible from the relevant literature on the subject: "Islamic economics aims at the study of human *falāḥ* achieved by organizing the resources of the earth on the basis of cooperation and participation".

The key concepts in the above definition are the following:

a) *falāḥ*;
b) resources; and
c) cooperation and participation.

2.1 *Falāḥ*

It is difficult to find a single equivalent for this term in the English language. The term *falāḥ* has been derived from the Arabic root *flḥ*. Its verbal form *aflaḥ, yufliḥu* means: to thrive; to become happy; to have good luck or success; to be successful. According to Rāghib al-Iṣfahāni, *falāḥ* is a both-worldly concept.[8] For the life in this world, it represents three things: *baqā'* (survival), *ghanā* (freedom from want) and *'izz* (power and honour). In the hereafter, it stands for: *bāqā' bilā fanā'* (eternal survival), *ghanā bilā faqr* (eternal prosperity), *'izz bilā dhull* (everlasting glory) and *'ilm bilā jahl* (knowledge free of all ignorance). According to the Qur'ān, the ultimate goal of human life should be the achievement of *falāḥ* in the hereafter. The life in the hereafter is a reality as compared to the life in this world, which has been declared by the Qur'ān to be merely a play and a passing delight. Although the ultimate object of Islamic economics is the achievement of *falāḥ* in the life to come, but it would be a reward for one's deeds during his stay in this world. *Falāḥ* in this world leads to the *falāḥ* in the hereafter. Conformity to the Islamic way of life is a means to achieve *falaḥ* both in this world and the hereafter. In the following discussion, we shall try to explore further the implications of *falāḥ* in this world.

In the context of this worldly life, *falāḥ* is a multi-dimensional concept. It has implications both for individual behaviour (micro-level) as well as for collective behaviour (macro-level). The following table summarizes the meanings of *falāḥ* at both the levels.

TABLE : 2

		Micro-level	Macro-level
FALĀḤ	Survival	Biological survival i.e. physical health, freedom from disease	Ecological balance, hygienic environment, and medical aid for all
		Economic survival i.e. having means of livelihood	Management of natural resources to generate work opportunities for the entire population
		Social survival i.e. brotherhood and harmonious inter-personal relationships	Inner social cohesion; absence of internecine conflicts among different groups
		Political survival i.e. freedom and participation in the affairs of the state	Independence and self-determinatio n as an entity
	Freedom from want	Alleviating poverty	Provisioning for the entire population
		Self-reliance i.e. work rather than parasitic idleness	Generating resources for the coming generations

		Micro-level	Macro-level
FALĀH	Power and Honour	Self-respect	Economic power and freedom from debt
		Civil liberties, protection of honour and life	Military power

It is obvious from the above table that *falāḥ* is a comprehensive concept and covers the whole of man's life. It is an ideal towards which Islam requires the human beings to strive. The Qur'ān has mentioned both positive and negative conditions for the achievement of *falāḥ*. In the Qur'ān the uses of the term *falāḥ* or its derivatives occur at forty places. A perusal of these verses leads us to determine the conditions of *falāḥ* at various levels.

2.1.1 Conditions of *Falāh*

The conditions of *falāh* may be categorized as below :

(a) spiritual,
(b) economic,
(c) cultural, and
(d) political.

(a) Spiritual Conditions of *Falāh*:

(i) Humility in prayers (*khushū'*),[9]
(ii) Consciousness of God (*taqwā*),[10]
(iii) Remembrance of God (*dhikr*),[11]
(iv) Repentance for sins (*tawbah*),[12]
(v) Inner purification (*tazkiyah*).[13]

Each one of these conditions is loaded with meaning. As the literature on Islamics contains comprehensive discourses on these aspects of *falāh* we shall not elaborate on them at this place.

(b) Economic Conditions of *Falāh*

(i) *Infāq*: *Infāq* refers to spending on others and on the social needs of the community merely to seek God's pleasure. This is something distinct from social alms which have been prevalent in all civilized societies. The pre-Islamic Arabs were also aware of charity. But Islam has broadened the concept of charity in a number of ways. First, it has made obligatory a bare minimum of social spending (called *zakāh*) on all those who have a surplus over and above their needs. To that extent, it is not voluntary. Second, in its broader meaning, *infāq* covers expenditure on one's own family as well which is not so in the case of charity. Third, Islam recognizes the right of the poor and the needy to receive a share from the wealth of the rich. The poor do not owe any obligation, moral or social, towards those who spend something on them. Fourth, *infāq* has to be purely for the sake of God who has promised reward in the hereafter. Charity in a secular society is usually done for winning social approbation rather than to seek God's pleasure. *Infāq* in the Islamic sense is a mechanism to nourish one's spirituality. This is one reason why secrecy in *infāq* is preferred, although its announcement to induce others to charitable spending is not prohibited.

The Qur'ān has laid down *infāq* as a condition to achieve *falāḥ*.[14] *Infāq* has to be only a part of one's total possessions. One is not required to spend the whole of his wealth. The Qur'ān says: "He does not demand of you (to sacrifice in His cause all of your possessions for) were He to demand of you all of them, and urge you, you would niggardly cling (to them) and then He would bring out your ill-feeling" (47:37).

The implication is that since man "has been created weak" (4:28) and since he has an inborn passion for wealth (100:8), he would be overburdened if asked to sacrifice everything in the cause of God. Thus the Qur'ān illustrates its deep awareness of human nature. By keeping *infāq* as a part of the total possessions, it has provided human beings with the incentive to strive and to generate a surplus to be passed on to future generations as well as to fulfil one's needs. It attaches a high priority to personal needs. *Infāq* is required from out of the surplus one has, and which one is required to devote to righteous purposes.[15] The famous commentator of the Qur'ān, Maḥmūd 'Ālūsī (d.1270 H.), has expressed the view that *infāq* of only a part of ones' possessions is sufficient to attain *falāḥ* and it is not necessary to spend the whole of one's wealth.[16] The reason is that such an action would lead to monasticism. It is in this context that we should view the fact that the Prophet (peace be upon him) asked one of his companions not to spend the whole of his wealth in the cause of God.[17]

Zakāh is part of the broader concept of *infāq*. The Qur'ān specifically enumerates *zakāh* as a condition of *falāḥ* presumably to emphasize its purifying role.[18] The underlying idea is that *zakāh* 'purifies' an individual's soul from excessive love for wealth.

Infāq implies a number of other traits of character. For example, *infāq* is possible for most people only when they adopt a simple life or else they would hardly be able to generate a surplus out of which a part might by transferred to others. Because human wants multiply fast. No sooner one satisfies a want than another crops up. It is only a simple and contented life which allows one to spare something for others. Therefore, the virtues of contentment, sacrifice, and moderation are natural corollaries of *infāq*. Similarly, an ostentatious and extravagant living is a hindrance to *infāq*. Whenever one cultivates the habit of *infāq* one has to adopt the overall life-style of Islam.

(ii) **Prohibition of Interest**: The Qur'ān declares interest on loan capital (*ribā*) as a hindrance to the achievement of *falāḥ*.[19] Interest on loan capital was prevalent in the pre-Islamic Arabian society. The wealthy exploited the poor and the needy. The custom of paying and receiving interest on commercial credit was also known to the Quraysh.[20] The Prophet (peace be upon him) declared all forms of interest as unlawful. He took various preventive measures as well so as to forestall the infiltration of interest into the economy in disguised forms.

The literature on Islamic economics discusses the prohibition of interest more than any other subject. It would be unnecessary to reproduce that material here in any detail. The main point that has been emphasized is that interest is a potent means for perpetrating exploitation and inequity. The road to *falāḥ* would remain blocked until interest is completely eliminated from the economy.

(iii) **Fulfillment of Covenants and Trusts**: Fulfillment of covenants and trusts is a necessary condition for *falāḥ*.[21] In its simple meaning it stands for honouring personal commitments and promises. But some scholars have placed a broader interpretation on the Qur'ānic teaching of fulfilling covenants. According to them, it involves meeting all one's social and religious obligations. One is obligated to obey God and His Messenger. One also has obligations towards the family, neighbours and the society.

From this they argue that polluting the environment through industrial waste contravenes one's obligations towards the society and hence retards the social pace towards *falāḥ*. Similarly, the government has the obligation to ensure welfare of the people. The society cannot achieve *falāḥ* until its inhabitants fulfil these implicit covenants.[22]

(iv) **Justice**: The Qur'ān has pleaded for justice at a number of places. It has linked *falāḥ* with the observance of justice in all affairs. The Qur'ān uses the term *ẓulm* (inequity) as an antonym of justice. The Qur'ān repeats that the *ẓālim* (one who perpetrates *ẓulm*) would not achieve *falāḥ*.[23] A society in which one's lawfully acquired wealth is appropriated by others without any compensation or consideration would suffer from wide inequalities, impaired incentives and social waste. Islamic law has clearly defined the lawful means of acquiring wealth. Digression from these means would amount to *ẓulm* and would hinder the way to *falāḥ*.

(v) **Enterprise**: God speaks of enterprise and struggle for livelihood as "seeking His bounty". Enterprise and effort to harness natural resources are an essential condition to achieve *falāh*. The Qur'ān says: "And when the prayer ends disperse freely on earth and seek to obtain (something) of God's bounty, but remember God often, so that you might attain *falāḥ*" (62:10).

Although there are a number of other verses which exhort man to "seek the bounty of God", in the present verse that exhortation is also suffixed by the prospect of achieving *falāḥ*. This ties in quite appropriately with the Prophet's statements urging people to work so as to earn their livelihood, his condemnations of idleness and beggary, his instructions to develop the land and to use the natural resources intensively, and his good tidings for the merchants and craftsmen. Thus the productive economic activity contributes to the *falāh* of the society as well as of the individual.

(c) Cultural Conditions of *Falāḥ*

The Qur'ān visualizes a certain cultural pattern for the Muslims. Unless the society adopts this pattern it would not attain *falāḥ*. We shall describe the cultural conditions of *falāḥ* briefly since details have been amply illustrated in the writings of the Muslim economists.

i) ***System of Prayers* (*Iqāmat al-ṣalāh*)**: It covers the establishment of mosques, arrangements for congregational prayers — both daily and weekly — and the appointment of the mosque staff, etc. The Islamic system of prayers five times a day is the manifestation of — highly disciplined activity. People line up behind a leader and offer the prayer in an organized manner. It seems that besides other benefits the obligatory prayers are a mechanism to teach discipline and organization to the individuals.

(ii) **Knowledge *('ilm)***: The Qur'ān repeatedly says that the fabricators of lies would not attain *falāḥ*.[24] This explains the emphasis of the Qur'ān on inquiry and pursuit of knowledge. The Qur'ān has also condemned sorcery and remarked that sorcerers would not achieve *falāḥ*.[25] The Qur'ān visualizes a society where people would base their actions on knowledge rather than superstitions and myths. In the same vein, the Qur'ān condemns lottery and idolatry.[26] It is obvious, therefore, that a society which ignores the pursuit of knowledge would not attain *falāḥ*.

(iii) **Sexual Chastity:** The Qur'ān has enumerated sexual chastity and modesty as one of the characteristics of those who attain *falāḥ*.[27] Legitimate sexual relations are a foundation stone of a stable family life. However, when the sexual desire exceeds its legitimate limits, it leads to anarchy, broken homes, juvenile delinquency and venereal diseases.

(iv) **Prohibition of Drinking Alcohol and Gambling:** Drinking of alcohol and other intoxicants and playing games of chance lead to numerous social evils. The Qur'ān holds them to be obstacles to *falāḥ*.[28]

(v) **Purification of the Environment**: The Qur'ān speaks of inner purification (*tazkiyah*) as a major condition for *falāḥ*.[29] Although this is often taken to mean inner purity (or *zakāh*) from wealth, some scholars have extended it to the purification of the environment.[30] This interpretation seems plausible if we were to look at the Qur'ānic emphasis on cleanliness of body and clothes. The pollution of the environment caused by the contemporary scramble for material development does not fit well into the Islamic concept of *falāḥ*.

(vi) **Enjoining the Proper and Forbidding the Improper**: One of the distinctive features of the Islamic economy is that every individual is responsible for enjoining the proper behaviour and forbidding the improper one. The Qur'ān considers this to be an important condition for attaining *falāḥ*.[31] The Islamic society builds a social conscience which tends to prevent people from improper behaviour. The members of one's family and the people around in the community keep an eye on the undesirable conduct of the individuals and try to control it. It is very rare that the government has to invoke the law to elicit proper behaviour from the individuals.

(vii) **Keeping Away from Frivolities**: The Qur'ān enjoins that wasting time on frivolous pursuits is a hurdle to achieving *falāḥ*. This implies utilizing one's time, effort and resources on useful and productive avenues.[32]

(d) Political Conditions of *Falāḥ*

(i) **Striving in the Cause of God (Jihād)**: The main political condition for *falāḥ* is striving in the cause of God.[33] In its narrow sense, striving in the cause of God stands for armed struggle against injustice and to protect the weak from the powerful. In its broader sense, it covers all efforts to propagate and enforce justice and fairplay and the sovereignty of God. It includes help and solace to the people in distress anywhere in the world.

(ii) **Role of State**: Another condition on the political front is the commitment of the government to provide basic necessities of life to its entire population, to protect the life, honour and property of the people, to involve people in the affairs of the state and to inculcate a sense of accountability both to man and to God for its policies and programmes. These conditions are derived from the general conditions of fulfilling the covenants discussed above.

In brief, *falāḥ* is a multi-dimensional concept. It covers the whole life of an individual and all aspects of a society. Its different conditions reinforce and supplement each other. Establishing a socio-economic institutional framework facilitates its achievement. The role of government can also be very important in promoting *falāḥ* of the people. Without this collective effort, the individual members of the society can hardly achieve *falāḥ* in the present world. For example, if a society does not collectively eliminate interest, it becomes very difficult for individuals to abstain from it.

Islamic economics concentrates on the economic dimension of *falāḥ*. Obviously, it requires the insights of religious scholars, sociologists, political scientists, psychologists, etc., to define the operational parameters of *falāḥ*. Islamic economics cannot analyze *falāḥ* by just taking into account the economic behaviour of the individuals.

Falāḥ does not consist merely of alleviation of poverty and freedom from want. This is only one aspect of it. *Falāḥ* implies reshaping human behaviour in the light of Islamic norms and values, alongside providing a reasonable standard of living and clean environment for everyone. It also suggests developing self-reliant, self-respecting and God-conscious individuals. It visualizes a high degree of individual and collective discipline cultivated through a system of daily prayers and worship. Love for knowledge, spirit of scientific and objective inquiry and keeping away from frivolous things are other traits of human character which promote *falāḥ*. Although Islamic economics is mainly concerned with one aspect of *falāḥ* — that which pertains to the production, distribution and exchange of resources — yet it studies it in the overall matrix of human behaviour.

2.2 Resources

The second key concept in the definition of Islamic economics is "resources" of the earth. God has created these resources for all human beings and has made man their trustee. God would like man to use these resources to achieve *falāḥ*. Islamic economics studies human behaviour towards these resources and investigates those modes of their development and use which lead to *falāḥ*. Since man is not the real owner of these resources he is not independent in deriving benefit from them. He is required to harness them according to the directives of God. Moreover, God has created everything on this earth with a purpose. The resources of the earth are meant to provide livelihood to the creatures of God. Therefore, no one should block these resources, depriving his own self as well as others of their use. The overall spirit of Islam is that either one should use the resources one has come to possess or release them for others.

The Qur'ān informs us that God has created sufficient resources for His creatures.[34] Therefore, the apparent scarcity of resources may be either due to their improper use or imbalanced distribution. Islamic economics studies resources from the point of view of '*adequacy*' rather than scarcity. It is not the main object of Islamic economics to study the allocation of '*scarce*' resources on multiple ends which is the focus of mainstream economics. Islamic economics is mainly concerned with the *falāḥ* of the people. It starts from the premise that the natural resources of the earth are adequate to achieve *falāḥ*. Therefore, if some degree of '*scarcity*' is being encountered, ways and means should be found to restore the natural state of adequacy. This could probably be achieved by broadening the productive base, improving technical know-how, re-distributing the resources or curtailing human wants. Scarcity of resources is a man-made situation and Islamic economics explores the ways and means to rectify it. .

There is also a moral dimension to this question. Man is accountable for his deeds in the hereafter. He will also be held accountable for the manner in which he uses these resources. Islam lays down standards of propriety for acquisition, utilization and transfer of resources. These standards have a high moral content. Islamic economics takes into account these standards and judges human behaviour in their light.

2.3 Cooperation and Participation

Islam emphasizes cooperation among human beings. Co-operation, from an Islamic viewpoint, appears more in line with the broader cosmic phenomenon of the entire universe. Nature makes a magnificent display of harmony and cooperation. A pervasive harmony is visible in the drama of creation, evolution, growth, decay and death followed by regeneration that keeps on going. In fact, the phenomenon is so obvious that the Qur'ān has mentioned it as a sign of the unity of God (*tawhīd*). The Qur'ān says: "Verily, your Sustainer is God, Who has created the heavens and the earth in six aeons, and is established on the Throne. He covers the day with night in swift pursuit, with the sun and the moon and the stars subservient to His command..."(7:54). The Qur'ān portrays an ordered universe of which each part co-operates with the other:

> ... (and) neither may the sun overtake the moon, nor can the night usurp the day since all of them are afloat through space [in accordance with Our laws]" (36:40).

On the human plane, God has created natural inequalities in resource endowments so as to foster mutual cooperation. Men have been created unequal in various respects. People differ in respect of physical attraction, knowledge, wealth, power, psychic traits and everything else that one may think of. The divine scheme is that none should be completely independent of others. In fact no civilized life is conceivable if people do not cooperate with one another. The Qur'ān emphasizes the same fact when it says:

> (Nay,) it is We Who distribute their means of livelihood among them in the life of this world, and raise some of them by degrees above others, to the end that they might avail themselves of one another's help ... (43:32).

This natural phenomenon extends to the sphere of human behaviour as well. Inter-personal relationships in Islam are based on the concept of the universal brotherhood of all human beings.[35] Human beings are conceived to be like the organs of a body, so that the whole body should sense pain if any organ suffers from discomfort.[36] Islamic social norms prescribe a high level of personal sacrifice for others. The Qur'ān has explicitly ordained that people should help one another in furthering God-consciousness (*taqwā*) and social virtue (*birr*).[37] Islamic values define social virtue to consist of a number of noble acts which, of course, includes rendering people economic assistance. Thus mutual help rather than conflict should be the basis of all economic relationships. The Qur'ān says:

> For He (it is) Who, after creating the earth, placed firm mountains on it, (towering) above its surface and bestowed (so many) blessings on it, and equitably apportioned its means of subsistence to all who would seek it: (and all this He created) in four aeons"(41:10).

Thus, the resources of the earth have been created for all the creatures of God and the natural scheme is that of *'participation'* of all in the utilization of these resources. The Qur'ān pleads for participation in economic endowments to modify the flow of resources generated by socio-economic conditions over a long period. It exhorts people to set aside a part of their resource-endowment for others who are deprived. The whole idea is quite simple. Those who have resources surplus to their basic needs have, somehow, received a share which should have gone to others, a desirable state of affairs which has been prevented by faulty socio-economic conditions. To rectify this maldistribution they should now voluntarily make it possible for others to share in them.

It was this spirit of *'participation'* that the Prophet (peace be upon him) tried to inculcate when he exhorted people to share their surplus food, housing, mount and land with others.[38] He praised the tribe of Ash'ar because they used to pool their foodstuff and distribute them in times of food shortages.[39] His decision to distribute the funds of *fay'* and poll-tax among the people is also an indication of the Prophet's strong preference for *'participation'* of the people in the resources. We learn from a number of traditions that the Prophet (peace be upon him) would not let any time pass before he distributed the wealth received in the public exchequer.[40] The Qur'ānic injunctions about the distribution of war booty also point to the participation of all combatants and non-combatants in it. The Prophet (peace be upon him) distributed the state's share in the war booty among the poor and the needy although they had not actively participated in the war. Similarly, the Qur'ānic injunction to spend in the cause of God whatever one can spare (2:219) also points to the desirable objective of sharing the surplus with others.

More specifically, Islam carries the same spirit of cooperation and participation into various laws regulating the economic behaviour. The law of *zakāh* which gives the poor a share in the wealth of the rich is an obvious example. The cornerstone of the Islamic business law is that the entitlement to gain is bound with one's acceptance of liability for loss, if any. Any business contract which involves one's exclusive entitlement to gain without his sharing the risk is unlawful. Similarly, those contracts which aim at a definite gain for one party and a definite loss for the other are void. The main current in the business law is the spirit of mutual help, gain and participation. Contracts that are likely to generate dispute owing to indefinite or undefined elements are prohibited since they may lead to exploitation of one party by another.

These concerns are also evident from the Islamic standpoint on interest. One of the main reasons for prohibiting interest is that the creditor's right to receive interest is assured irrespective of the fact that his capital has added any value or not. There is hardly any difference of opinion on the prohibition of interest regarding consumption loans, since it involves brazen exploitation of the poor. But some people have tried to argue that interest on productive loans is not prohibited as in this case the lender shares the profit of the borrower which he makes by using the capital made available to him by the lender. But the main fallacy in the argument lies in fixing a rate of interest without ascertaining the extent of profit that the capital may or may not generate. A more rational and consistent approach would be that the capital should participate in the production process as an equal partner, and not as a *'superior'* one entitled to a fixed return on capital. As a result of business operations, all the factors of production should share the net contribution in a mutually agreed proportion. Because of this inherent inconsistency, interest has been prohibited, since its permissibility would lead to serious inner conflicts and contradictions in the economic system.

A number of scholars have emphasized the desirability of labour sharing the profit. The suggestions are justified on ground of the various traditions about showing benevolence to the slave-labour.

Even if we may dismiss the analogy of slave-labour with the wage-labour as remote and irrelevant, it seems that the Prophet (peace be upon him) envisaged that the economic system should preferably be based on cooperation and participation. He did not suggest that the status of slaves should be raised to that of wage-earners. He rather made them 'equals' on the basis of fraternity and fellow-feeling. The wage-labour retains the concept of pre-determined wage-rate for the workers irrespective of the fact that the enterprise creates additional wealth or not. But the participation of workers in the net contribution visualizes organization of the economy on the principles of cooperation and participation.

3. SOURCES OF ISLAMIC ECONOMICS

The guiding principles of Islamic economics are derived from the follow sources:

a) The Qur'ān;
b) The *Sunnah* of the Prophet (peace be upon him);
c) Islamic Law and Jurisprudence;
d) History of the Muslims; and
e) Data Relating to Economic Life.

(a) The Qur'ān

The Qur'ān is the book of God which has been preserved since it was revealed. The Qur'ān contains general and broad guidelines for the conduct of human beings. On economic matters, too, it provides a set of fundamental principles to guide human conduct. Consistent with these principles, the superstructure of the economy has to be built, in each age, according to the particular circumstances of each age. The injunctions of the Qur'ān are immutable and applicable to all societies and are valid for all times to come. The Qur'ān is thus a primary source of Islamic economics.

(b) The Sunnah of the Prophet (peace be upon him)

The *sunnah* is the speech, action or tacit approval of the Prophet (peace be on him) as recorded in the books of traditions. The compilers of these traditions have analyzed, classified and interpreted the whole material. The literature on traditions of the Prophet (peace be upon him) covers the entire orbit of life, including the economic aspect. Although most of the traditions are general and applicable for all times there are some whose relevance is time-bound. Therefore, the knowledge of the exact status of each tradition is essential to understand its relevance for the present age. Knowledge of the traditions containing injunctions about economic activities is an essential part of the training of Muslim economists.[41]

(c) Islamic Jurisprudence

There exists a vast legal literature developed by the Muslim jurists over the last fourteen centuries. It deals with the formalization of the injunctions of the Qur'ān and the traditions of the Prophet (peace be upon him). A large part also deals with those questions which arose subsequent to the Prophet's time. The jurists have been elaborating and deriving inferences about economic questions as well. In fact some of the early works of jurisprudence deal with finance and land management. These discussions have a variety of shades and their perusal opens a wide span of subjects which have been of interest to jurists of each age. The different juridical opinions carry an explicit note illuminating the circumstances in which those opinions were expressed.

Islamic economics draws heavily on this rich heritage. But the opinions of the jurists are not inviolable and can be modified and adjusted according to the changed circumstances. Islamic economics studies the impact of these legal opinions on the behaviour of the people. The Muslim economists try to formulate theories in the light of the vast body of juridical opinions.

The Muslim economists visualize elaboration, extension and reconsideration of the earlier legal works. The questions which the contemporary scene has thrown up have to be studied to arrive at a competent legal position. Collaboration of religious scholars with economists is, thus, a necessity for the development of Islamic economics.

(d) **History of the Muslims**

The history of the Muslims contains much scattered material about the economic life of the people. These parts of the history serve as useful precedents for the present-day economy. Although most of what prevailed then has undergone a metamorphosis yet the early precedents lend useful insights for the application of the Islamic economic system in the contemporary setting. The economic history of the Muslims has not yet been chronicled except for some elementary accounts of the early period. We hope that with the growth of the subject the historical sources will also develop.

(e) **Real Life Data**

This is the main area of operation for a Muslim economist. He studies the real life conditions and behaviour of the people and uses the available data for analysis and formulation of policies. The 'real life data' here refers to the objective conditions prevailing in an economy. None of the present day economies are Islamic in the real sense. They have adopted various patterns of capitalism and socialism. Islamic economics aims at the transformation of the present day economies, which are full of shortcomings from an Islamic viewpoint, into truly 'Islamic' economies. For this purpose it focuses on the development of strategies for transition. To that extent the study of the actual conditions of the contemporary times becomes necessary and is in fact an integral part of Islamic economics.

The main concern of Islamic economics, however, remains the achievement and maintenance of *falāḥ*. The real life data as a source of Islamic economics means the study of the impact of various Islamic injunctions on the behaviour of various economic variables and the effort to develop ideas for transforming them in the light of Islamic norms.

4. THE APPROACH OF ISLAMIC ECONOMICS

How does Islamic economics approach its subject-matter? We shall discuss the methodology of Islamic economics in chapter three. But for now, we shall confine ourselves to making a brief exposition of the Islamic approach to economic matters.

The method of Islamic economics presumes a primary and binding role for the ideological content. The basic premises are defined by the Islamic law. The Muslims economists develop their analysis by employing reason and real life data to the divinely ordained content of Islam. Islamic economics cannot be conceived outside this basic framework.

Islamic economics conceives human behaviour in its totality. It treats human life as a compact whole which is composed of multiple mutually-reinforcing sub-systems. The economic sub-system is one of these sub-systems. It is not even the central sub-system. It affects the human behaviour only from the periphery. The hard core of the system is composed of the basic beliefs in the Unity of God, in the apostle-hood of Muḥammad (peace be upon him) and in man's accountability on the Day of Judgement. These beliefs are the foundation of each sub-system.

The hard core radiates the fundamental principles of behaviour and moulds human attitude in all the sub-systems. Between themselves the sub-systems are open and interact. But each sub-system also has a composition of its own which aims at the achievement of *falāḥ*. The economic sub-system consists of legal foundation of justice (*'adl*) and ethical foundation of moderation (*iqtiṣād*) and benevolence (*iḥsān*). The legal foundation ordains legal and contractual relationships. Although Islam has a mature and comprehensive legal system, yet the total area of human behaviour covered by the legal injunctions is rather small. A very wide area of human behaviour consists of voluntary acts. The voluntary acts are influenced by considerations of moderation and benevolence. Moderation is the mother-norm and governs individual behaviour towards one's ownself. Benevolence is a cluster of ethical precepts and influences inter-personal relationships.

Fig. 1 below illustrates the holistic vision of human behaviour and the place of the economic sub-system in it.

HOLISTIC VISION OF HUMAN BEHAVIOUR

Fig. 1.

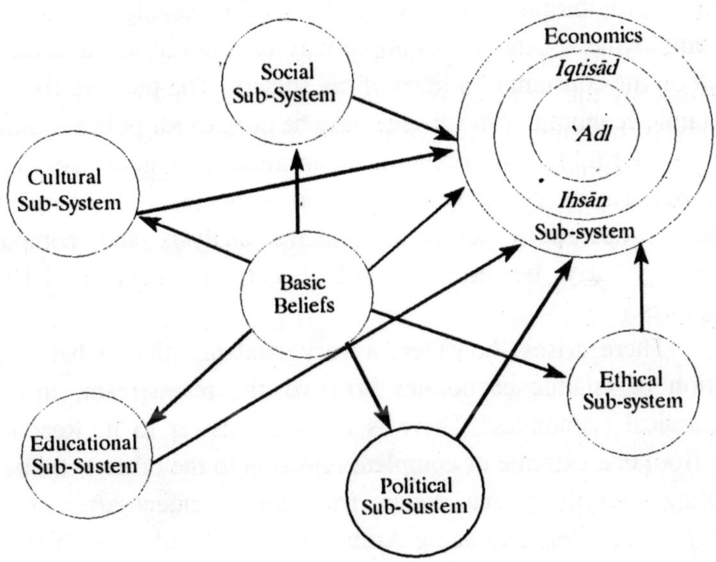

Islamic economics takes into account the economic behaviour of man in the context of his overall conduct. It does not restrict itself to the 'market' variables. Instead, it integrates the findings of other social sciences into its subject-matter. In sum, the approach of Islamic economics is interdisciplinary.

Second, a very high content of Islamic economics is normative. The Muslim economists have the obligation to discharge the Qur'ānic duty of enjoining what is proper and forbidding what is improper. Therefore, Islamic economics studies and suggests ways and means for achieving *falāḥ*. It makes note of the deviations from the basic Islamic framework in human behaviour and devises policies for attaining a higher level of conformity. Islamic economics plans to foretell the possible economic crises that might develop as a result of aberrant behaviour of the economic actors. It suggests suitable policy measures to prevent crises before they actually develop.

Third, despite being highly normative, Islamic economics has a vast positive content as well. It attempts to study the impact and reaction of various legal injunctions and ethical values on the economic variables. For example, it may be of interest to study the effect of prohibition of interest on the level of savings, investment and employment. Another example may be a study of the effect of *zakāh* on the consumption level of the society. The positive findings of Islamic economics can subsequently be utilized for policy-making.

Fourth, Islamic economics can also make good use of the tools of analysis developed by modern economics. Mathematics, statistics, operations research, systems analysis and computer technology may be utilized with benefit to develop Islamic economics.

There arises, however, a very vital question: what is the position of Islamic economics *vis-ā-vis* the mainstream, that is, neoclassical economics? There is no final answer to it. Reactions vary from one extreme of complete rejection to the other extreme of adopting everything that comes from the Occident after simply changing the labels and using Arabic equivalents of English terms. We believe that both the extremes represent unbalanced approaches. A more moderate approach is the one pleaded for by Ism'ail R. al-Fārūqī, under the general rubric of Islamization of knowledge. According to this approach, the task before Islamic economics would be to study the mainstream economics critically, identify its assumptions and values, sift what may be termed as fully established facts of economic life from the merely tentative hypotheses or theories based on insufficient evidence, and to synthesize these facts into the Islamic worldview. Although the general case for this approach is quite persuasive, the difficulty with the approach is that it takes the researcher into an endless race of keeping a track of the knowledge in the West and modifying his own work in its light. It is a never-ending race in which the Muslim economist always remains behind the Western secular economist.

A more promising approach, in our view, is being pleaded by a group which calls itself the Ijmālīs, the group of intellectuals consisting of such persons as Pervaiz Manzoor, Ziauddin Sardar and Munawar Ahmad Anees. They visualize the development of Islamic disciplines in the light of the Islamic worldview without getting into the business of developing a critique of Western knowledge. Nevertheless, they would also like to use the real life data in developing Islamic disciplines.

At this stage we need to mention a trap into which many Muslim economists have landed themselves. The economic thought developed by the Occident overpowers their reasoning and they are persuaded by its 'truth'. Then they try to interpret the texts of the Qur'ān and the *Sunnah* in such a manner as would accommodate the secular economic thought of the Occident. They start reading the findings of the secular economists into these primary sources. While there is no bar on the interpretation of the Qur'ān and the *Sunnah* in each age, the danger is that this approach might reduce the entire discipline of Islamic economics into a sterile intellectual exercise, to a sheer act of mimicry, or at least to turn Islamic economics into a sub-discipline of secular economics, thus robbing it of its identity and uniqueness. If that happens, the original objectives of developing Islamic economics would be defeated. There is no hard and fast rule for remaining out of this trap except that the Muslim economists should widely discuss their ideas. It is only through a process of self-criticism that they can guard themselves against this trap.

Three

METHODOLOGY OF ISLAMIC ECONOMICS

1. INTRODUCTION

The main objective of the present chapter is to discuss in broad and general terms the methodology of Islamic economics and to show in what respects it differs from the methodology of the mainstream economics. We shall also take up, in this chapter, some related issues such as the Islamic approach towards the mainstream economics, the roles of revelation and reason, and the assumption of an ideal Islamic society in Islamic economics. We do not intend, however, to discuss or appraise the methodology of the mainstream economics. A vast literature already exists on this subject[1] and its restatement here would be hardly of any substantial benefit. In this section we intend to take up two questions: first, why do we discuss the methodology of a subject especially that of economics? Second, why do we need a methodology for Islamic economics?

1.1 Why Methodology at all?

The methodology of a subject critically investigates the concepts, theories and basic principles of reasoning pertaining to that subject.[2] There is a wide difference of opinion concerning the methodology of economics. From the classical emphasis on the verification of assumptions to the neoclassical falsification of predictions, the debate on methodology touches upon such issues as positive versus normative, inductive versus deductive, incorporation of values versus exclusion of values, prescription versus description, apriorism versus empiricism, to name only some of the main questions currently under discussion. Economists have taken positions on these issues and often heated debates have ensued as a result. The question arises: why should there be any discussion of methodology at all? The answer is that economists are keen to reach the truth and each methodological approach claims to reach it in a surer manner as compared to the others.[3] Looking from this angle, the debate on methodology is an inborn human demand. Man has been keen to reach the truth in all ages. The Qur'ān also invites people to its message on the plea that it is a Book of sure knowledge.[4] Thus it appeals to the human instinct to reach the truth. The Qur'ān argues that one should discard the doubtful against the sure.[5] The debate on methodology in economics and other sciences as well shows that there is hardly a disagreement on this basic fact. The entire debate is intended to establish clear and consistent rules to sift the true from the false.

1.2 Need for Defining the Methodology of Islamic Economics

Despite the differences in the various strands of methodological debate in economics there is a broad agreement on at least three points concerning human beings:

(i) that they are mainly driven by their self-interest and that they tend to behave rationally;

(ii) that material progress is the supreme goal of their efforts; and

(iii) that human beings have an inherent tendency to maximize their material welfare and that they also have the knowledge and ability to decide what is good for them.

The Islamic viewpoint is quite different on these matters. First, it is questionable that human beings are selfish by nature. There is overwhelming evidence that in all civilized societies people have been actuated by altruistic motives. Altruism is as much a fact of life as is selfishness. Islam encourages people to adopt altruism and to make sacrifice for others.[7] The Qur'ān has praised those Muslims who prefer to fulfil the needs of others although they are in difficulty.[8] Caring for others is a paramount value inculcated by Islam. Muslim societies have a history of *waqf* institutions devoted to philanthropic activities.[9] Even in this age when the religious loyalty seems to have somewhat weakened, people in the Muslim societies display a spirit of altruism. In non-Muslim societies too philanthropy is a fact of life. Only in America twenty two thousand organizations are engaged in philanthropic activities.[10] In sum, the assumption about the selfish nature of man is not supported by the evidence drawn from actual life.

Second, material progress is not a supreme objective in an Islamic society.[11] As discussed in chapter two, it is a desirable goal but is subservient to the *falāḥ* in the hereafter, should there be a conflict. The Prophet (peace be upon him) led a simple life and his companions too lived with simplicity. The Qur'ān talks of worldly life as a plaything and a fleeting joy. It seems that the primary emphasis is on the well-being of man in the hereafter. This does not mean that Islam teaches monasticism or fatalism.[12] Far from that, it enjoins upon its followers a balanced attitude. Material prosperity is desirable in so far as it helps one to perform one's duties to God, society, family and one's own self.[13] It should be a means to achieve *falāh* in the hereafter. Taking up material progress as the supreme objective of life is thus alien to the Islamic vision of life.

Third, Islam considers man incapable of knowing independently what is best for him.[14] Only God has perfect knowledge. Human knowledge is imperfect and every person needs guidance for making various decisions in life. God, in His infinite mercy, has revealed His guidance for the benefits of human beings through the Prophets and His Books.

Thus, Islamic economics has a different position on the basic assumptions of the mainstream economics. This provides, in part, the need and justification for a separate methodology of Islamic economics. There is another difficulty with the mainstream economics. It does not accept any source of knowledge other than human knowledge, which is derived through the mental hypothetic-deductive processes. Thus it has closed upon itself the doors of the sure knowledge available from the divine source. This has not only increased the confusion found in the realm of economic thinking but has also left the question of criteria for truth unsettled. As a result, there is hardly anything in the mainstream economics which is universally accepted as valid and true. It seems that the entire knowledge of economics has been developed for its own sake and not for the sake of humanity.[15] The complete denial of any knowledge derived from the divine source has left economics without any universally accepted framework. Almost everything is questionable.

This is not to contend that the process of criticism and rational examination of economic theories itself is questionable. It only means that economics does not have any hard core of sure knowledge which may be treated as the ultimate point of reference and criterion for judging the truth and falsity of various theories. Therefore, there is a need for developing a methodology which not only provides a basis for sure knowledge but also eliminates the existing confusion by laying down a criterion for judging the contending theories. Islamic economics derives these criteria from the revealed knowledge.

2. METHODOLOGY OF ISLAMIC ECONOMICS

2.1 The Hard Core

The basic function of methodology is to help man in reaching the truth. The hard core of Islamic economics consists of the postulates of the Qur'ān and the *Sunnah* of the Prophet (peace be upon him).

These postulates are of divine provenance. Therefore, the question of their truth or falsity does not arise. They are true because of their divine origin. The method of Islamic economics is that for each situation, reference is made to these two sources. It is only when no guidance is available in these sources that human reason comes in and the question of methodology arises. For example, a number of verses in the Qur'ān lay down general principles and predictions relating to the economic phenomena. We shall cite some of these verses below. These verses need no verification or confirmation because they have been revealed by the All-knowing God. In Islamic economics they are accepted as given. These and other verses of the Qur'ān and the authentic traditions of the Prophet (peace be upon him) form the hard core of Islamic economics:

(i) God deprives usurious gains of all blessing whereas He blesses charitable deeds with manifold increase (2:276).

(ii) And if they would but truly observe the Torah and the Gospel, and all [the revelation] that has been sent down to them by their Sustainer, they would indeed partake of all the blessings of the heavens and the earth (5:66).

(iii) Then, when they had forgotten all that they had been told to take to heart, We threw open to them the gates of all (good) things, until — even as they were rejoicing in what they had been granted — We suddenly took them to task: and lo! they were broken in spirit (6:44).

(iv) Ask your Sustainer to forgive you your sins, and then turn towards Him in repentance (whereupon) He will grant you a goodly enjoyment of life (in this world) until a term set (by Him is fulfilled); and (in the Life to come) He will bestow upon everyone possessed of merit a full reward for this merit. But if you turn away, then, verily I dread for you the suffering (which is bound to befall you) on that Awesome Day (11:3).

(v) Hence, O my people, ask your Sustainer to forgive you your sins, and then turn towards Him in repentance — (whereupon) He will shower upon you heavenly blessings abundant, and will add strength to your strength (11:52).

(vi) If you are grateful (to Me), I shall most certainly give you more; but if you are ungrateful, verily, My chastisement will be severe indeed (14:7).

(vii) But for him who shall turn away from remembering Me — his shall be a life of narrow scope (20:124).

All these verses state a set of general economic principles and also make certain predictions. These predictions need no verification. They are true and Islamic economics accepts them as given. The hard core of Islamic economics consists of such axioms. They define the boundary conditions of Islamic economics. At the same time, they serve as the criteria for testing theories propounded by human beings. Any theory put forward by a person is tested on these criteria and if there is a clear and undeniable contradiction, the theory is rejected straightaway without any further examination.

The above methodology applies, however, only to the divine texts but not to the human interpretations of these texts. The human interpretations of these texts are open to examination and criticism. There exists a well formulated methodology (*'ilm al-ūsūl*) to derive inferences from these texts. The Islamic economist applies the same methodology for testing inferences from, and interpretations of, the divine texts. It is pertinent to add that the methodology to interpret the Qur'ān and the traditions of the Prophet (peace be upon him) also requires re-thinking. The early religious scholars of Islam showed remarkable insight, imagination and vision and interpreted the basic sources in the context of their times. With the passage of time the methodology developed by them seems to have lost some of its relevance due to changes in the living conditions of the people. Therefore, there is a need to review the whole methodology in the present age. For example, the traditions of the Prophet (peace be upon him) may be studied as a whole to understand the rationale and objectives of the Prophet (peace be upon him) on any particular issue. The insights thus gained should be used to determine the Islamic position on an analogous contemporary question. A host of new questions in the present day require an Islamic verdict but the Muslim scholars are unable to present an answer mainly because the existing methodology does not take them far enough. However, this is another subject and need not detain us at the moment.

2.2 The Role of Reason

The scope of Islamic economics includes a study of Islamic values, an analysis of real-life economic phenomena and an exploration of ways and means to transform the existing economies into an Islamic economy. Therefore, the hard core of Islamic economy provides direct guidance on a small number of questions. A dominant part of the economic reality requires the application of human reason and intellect within the over-all divine framework. The question of methodology arises mainly in the area where human reason is applied. In this area the general principle is that if a theory does not contradict any divine text, its soundness should be examined in the light of human reason.

This may be done by testing its validity on rational as well as empirical criteria. Every theory must satisfy both the criteria. It should be true on rational grounds and should also be confirmed by empirical evidence. Confirmation shall be sought by the Popperian thesis of falsification. It means that a theory would be tested on the criterion of falsifiability. The theories which are not falsified by these two criteria would be accepted. To this extent the methodology of Islamic economics is similar to that of the mainstream economics.

This further implies that the hypotheses of Islamic economics must be stated in a form that they may be discarded as false if they do not conform to the accepted criteria. In other words, a hypothesis must make clear its conditions and predictions. A hypothesis would merit consideration only if it indicates the situations in which it would not apply or if it specifies the conditions which would falsify it.

The falsifiability criterion applies only to the theories which discuss the how of an economic system. It does not apply to the questions of why in an economic system because reason can be applied only to questions of how. It cannot be applied to the questions of why which take one to the domain of faith and morality. In mainstream economics the questions which are asked are: how do markets behave? But one does not ask why they behave in a particular manner because this would drag economics into the domain of morality. Since Descartes, the Occident has learned to segregate reason from faith and morality. In Islamic economics, however, the questions of faith and morality are quite relevant. Therefore, in respect of the questions of why, Islamic economics applies the criteria of faith and morality.[18]

2.3 Inductive or Deductive Reasoning

What is the response of Islamic economics to the question of choice between inductive and deductive reasoning? The answer is that Islamic economics uses a combination of both the methods. But this brief answer needs qualification. Muslims are credited with contributing significantly to the development of inductive reasoning, and especially of the empirical method.[19] Before the advent of Islam the ancient world did produce some great systems of philosophy but they were largely based on abstract speculative reasoning.[20] The Qur'ān invited people to look and see. It argued on the evidence of such natural phenomena as sun, moon, day, night, rainfall, seasons, differences of colours and tongues.[21] This ignited a spirit of inquiry which led to the discovery of the inductive method in research. The Qur'ān cites the example of Prophet Abraham (AS) who asked for an empirical evidence for life after death.[22] Faith in One God in the case of Prophet Abraham (AS) also came by resorting to an empirical approach.[23] It is significant that the Qur'ān says: "Thus We showed to Abraham the visible and the invisible world of the heavens and the earth so that he could be among those who believe(6:75). Hence the emphasis on the word 'showed' (*nūrī*) refers to seeing and looking. God has referred to reasoning based on observation to establish the validity of metaphysical truths. This shows that for physical reality it would be still more preferable to hold on to this method.

Therefore, in Islamic economics the inductive method is only a continuation of the tradition set by the Muslims in the past. But it has been argued that it is not possible to derive any scientific conclusions merely by using the inductive method. The argument goes like this. Whenever a person looks around and sees a thing, there is always an *a priori* thought in his mind which makes him select the particular thing he saw out of the numerous others which he ignored. Therefore, the real source of knowledge is man's intellect and not observation. We do not dispute this argument. We accept that human intellect is the source of knowledge. But we would like to add that there are other sources of knowledge as well. For example, revelation and intuition are sources of knowledge.[24] Human mind is capable of receiving flashes of brilliant ideas which do not have any visible linkages in the empirical world or which are not the result of systematic observation. The point we want to make is that the source of a theory may be inductive or *a priori* but the Islamic economist would test it on the multiple criteria of divine texts, reason and empirical evidence.

Should we say, then, that Islamic economics does not use deductive reasoning at all? In our view, such a statement would not be meaningful unless it is subjected to qualifications. Deductive reasoning in economics assumes perfect knowledge of the future by economic agents. Abstract deductions are made on the basis of this assumption.[25] As a matter of fact, the whole corpus of economic theory mainly consists of deductions. The validity of the assumption of perfect knowledge has been called into question by empiricists. Islamic economics also cannot accept this assumption as it clashes with one of the fundamental beliefs of Islam. Perfect knowledge of the future is only with Allah and man's knowledge of it can only be partial and imperfect.[26] Therefore, the method of abstract deduction on the assumption of perfect knowledge cannot be acceptable to Islamic economics. The whole argument can now be summed up in one sentence. Islamic economics accepts human intellect as a valid source of knowledge but does not accept model-building on the basis of deductive reasoning. Model-building involves a series of deductions from initial premises, which assumes perfect knowledge of the future — an assumption which the Islamic economist tends to reject.

The question remains: How does Islamic economics proceed to model-building? Islamic economics accepts the real life situation that individuals do not have perfect fore-knowledge and different individuals have a knowledge which varies from the knowledge of others. Thus, in a given situation the possible reactions could be numerous. Hence, the only rational approach for Islamic economics is to observe the human behaviour in the historical and institutional setting and then hypothesis on the basis of actual knowledge. This would require adoption of unusual research methods borrowed from such disciplines as sociology, marketing, social psychology, social anthropology, history, business management and industrial relations. The sources of data would be as unusual as national accounts, company accounts, national budgets, trade practices, behaviour of employees, behaviour of farmers, etc.

2.4 Assumptions and Method

The basic assumptions of the mainstream economics have influenced its method as well. The economists tend to assumes that human beings are selfish and rational, that they seek maximization of their material well-being and that they possess the perfect knowledge of the future. These assumptions have led to the hypothetico-deductive method with a limited number of variables. Islamic economics does not agree with any of these assumptions.

In Islamic economics there are high-level assumptions derived from the divine texts and low-level assumptions based on human reasoning. The high-level assumptions need no verification. Therefore, Islamic economics dispenses with the need to discuss the validity or otherwise of these assumptions. But low-level assumptions need to be tested against the twin criteria of rationality and empirical evidence. This position is quite distinct from that of the mainstream economics. The mainstream economists have argued — the most prominent being Friedman — that the assumptions need not be empirically valid.[27] In fact, some have gone to the extent of saying that valid predictions are possible only from invalid assumptions. Islamic economics does not accept this position on the basis of rationality and empiricism.

This leads us to the question: what are high-level assumptions in Islamic economics? First, man is neither just selfish nor just altruistic; he is both.[28] He has an inborn tendency to be selfish and to love wealth but he has also been endowed with the ability of being altruistic. Caring for others is a trait of human character which can be verified by overwhelming real-life evidence. Second, altruistic behaviour can be cultivated and made persistent by education. Third, human beings have imperfect fore-knowledge.[29] Therefore, all economic analyses should be carried out in a world of uncertainty. Fourth, in the ultimate analysis, *falāḥ* in the hereafter is preferable to prosperity in the present world. This is not an exhaustive list of assumptions. More high-level assumptions can be developed on the basis of the teachings of the Qur'ān and the traditions of the Prophet (peace be upon him).

2.5 Problem-Solving

Islamic economic thought may be traced back to the early period of Islam. Thinkers of Islam like Abū Yūsuf, Abū 'Ubayd, Yaḥyā b. Ādam, Qudāmah b. Ja'far, al-Māwardī, al-Ghazālī, Ibn Taymiyah, Ibn Khaldūn, Shāh Walī Allāh, and thinkers of recent past like Iqbal, Muḥammad 'Abduh, Muḥammad Rashīd Riḍā, Mawdūdi, Bāqir al-Ṣadr, Ṭāliqānī, to name a few, have almost unanimously adopted a problem-solving approach.[31] They have been concerned about the economic problems of their respective times. They have written on poverty, social justice, taxation, economic balance, market imperfections and the allocative role of the state. They based their arguments on the worldview of Islam and brought rare insights to explain economic problems of their respective times. Islamic economics in our ages represents a continuation of this tradition. It studies the economic behaviour of individuals, households, firms and the state with the following focus:

(i) understanding the behaviour and decision-making processes;

(ii) relating human behaviour with the *falāḥ* of the owners, the employees, the clients, the citizens and the society at large; and

(iii) hypothesizing about alternative strategies to maximize *falāḥ* at different levels.

In order to illustrate, let us consider how a Muslim economist would deal with the question of firms. In our view, at the first stage a Muslim economist would attempt to understand how firms take various decisions regarding the production, pricing and marketing of their products. In this phase he may use with benefit the findings of neoclassical economics with the caveat that the assumptions of neoclassical economics might be unreal and over-simplified. Therefore, the Muslim economist might have to use other disciplines such as market research, production management and social psychology. At the second stage, he would relate his understanding with the *falāh* of the firms' owners, managers and ordinary citizens and he may point out the various trade-offs. At the third stage, he would try to build models which maximizes the *falāh* of the various economic agents.

Two conclusions, emerge from what we have said above:

(i) Islamic economics is a multi-disciplinary subject. It will not be meaningful nor would it achieve its objectives if it relies only on the traditional sources of economics.

(ii) Islamic economics is a normative discipline. It does not study the economic problem merely for the sake of knowing the economic problem. It has a normative purpose: to explore ways and means for transforming the existing economies into truly Islamic economies. The positive content of Islamic economics is neither underrated nor denied. The positive content is, however, used for normative purposes. Thus Islamic economics goes a step ahead of the mainstream economics.

2.6 Process of Theorizing

The process of theory-building in Islamic economics is different from what is commonly believed to be true for social sciences. In social sciences, like natural sciences, the researcher tries to arrive at the unknown from a known premise. But the fact is that this approach has not helped much in economics. The real life, however, is so complex that it is almost impossible to predict the outcome of a policy with any precision.

Islamic economics has inverted the whole process of Theorizing. It treats the future outcome as known. Its future outcome is the objective of achieving *falāḥ*. This is known. What is not known is the path through which we can attain the state of *falāḥ*. The role of economic theory comes at this stage.

The first task of theory is to devise one or more paths through which the initial state (or the present state) can be transformed into the terminal state (i.e. the state of *falāḥ*). By 'path' we mean a sequence of positions the system must assume on its way to the desired objective. Such positions can be described in terms of physical and price relations (such as inputs and outputs, income and employment, investment and consumption), or social variables (such as literacy rates, health facilities, crime rate) or spiritual variables (such as a person's attending the mosques regularly, the size and number of philanthropic institutions, the proportion of the people who perform pilgrimage, etc.). Once we know that path we can establish the behaviour pattern that will act as a force to set the system on the goal-adequate trajectory. Thus the behaviour pattern, although initially unknown, can be determined with the help of the knowledge of goal-adequate path and certain technological rules.

In this manner we can obtain knowledge of the structural and behavioural conditions suitable for the attainment of the goal. But we cannot assume that these suitable conditions coincide with actual conditions. This suggests that we shall have to visualize a set of public controls to elicit the suitable (or desirable) behaviour. These controls could be guideposts, persuasion, compensatory public spending, buffer stocks, wage, price, profit and investment controls and, in extreme cases, direct coercion as well. The exact set of controls to be followed will have to be identified by the economists in each case. In fact, one of the tasks of the theory is to identify the path, suitable behaviour patterns and a set of public controls to achieve the state of *falāḥ*.

3. COMPARISON OF THE TWO METHODOLOGIES

In this section we shall summarize our discussion of the previous section to highlight the distinctive features of Islamic economic methodology. First, Islamic economics uses a framework derived from the divine texts. This framework is sacred and immutable. No individual or group of individuals can make it redundant or irrelevant. Human criticism does not apply to the divine texts. This approach is quite distinct from that of the mainstream economics where the fundamental paradigm is also subject to criticism and can also undergo change.[32] However, the interpretations of the divine texts are not sacred, and thus not final and infallible. But the interpretations follow the methodology developed by Islamic scholars.

Second, Islamic economics primarily follows the inductive method. It testifies the truth or falsity of the assumptions as well as predictions on the twin criteria of rationality and empirical evidence. In the mainstream economics, the deductive method is more common. And as we know the assumptions of the economists need not always be realistic. The real test is the non-falsifiability of predictions. The basic assumptions of self-interest, rationality, perfect fore-knowledge, man's ability to know what is best for him have facilitated the use of the deductive method by economists. Islamic economics has a different stance on these issues. Therefore, it adopts a combination of inductive and deductive methods with primary emphasis on the former.

Third, Islamic economics builds ethical values such as justice, benevolence, moderation, sacrifice, caring for others, etc., into analysis as behavioural parameters. The debate whether economics should contain value judgements is a lengthy one. In the mainstream economics, the balance of the argument suggests that there is no escape from value judgements. But the economists should produce falsifiable hypothesis. In the process of hypothesis-testing, personal, social or political prejudices and value judgements should be eliminated. Herein lies the road to progress in economics. In Islamic economics, so far as the matter relates to personal choices, prejudices or preferences, this approach seems to be acceptable with an important qualification. The ethical values of Islam would continue to be part of economic theories and they would not be falsified by any hypothesis-testing along with the factual data. A theory which does not either incorporate any Islamic ethical norms or contradicts them or leads to predictions which would defeat or dilute the ethical norms would be rejected *per se* even in the absence of any empirical evidence.

Fourth, Islamic economics is a normative discipline. It explores the ways and means to change the existing economies into truly Islamic economies. Mainstream economics, on the other hand, claims to be a positive science which studies the existing economic phenomena without being overly concerned with altering that phenomena. Islamic economics, however, is interested in changing the economic reality. Its predictions relate to a world which has not yet been ushered in. Therefore, the actual testing of Islamic economic theories would wait until an Islamic economy comes into being. However, Islamic economics also concerns itself with the transition path. Its transition theories can be tested in the real world provided the process of transition sets in.

Fifth, Islamic economics asks questions which are different from those asked by the mainstream economics. It is concerned with the *falāḥ* of man, and with creating the social and institutional conditions which maximize *falāḥ* in a society. Implicitly, it visualizes pursuit of research programmes which contribute to the maximization of *falāḥ*. In this way, *falāḥ* becomes the criterion for acceptance or rejection of a research programme. In the mainstream economics no such criterion exists in unambiguous terms. As a result, it pursues research for the sake of research or knowledge for the sake of knowledge. In Islamic economics, all knowledge has a purpose. That purpose is derived from the over-all worldview of Islam.

4. SOME RELATED ISSUES

In this section we shall discuss some related issues which often come up for discussion in the forums of Islamic economics.

4.1 Role of Revelation

The general principle of Islamic methodology is that before anything else reference should be made to the Qur'ān and the *Sunnah* of the Prophet (peace be upon him) for seeking guidance on any issue. But there is a limit to what we can get from these sources. The Qur'ān and the traditions of the Prophet (peace be upon him) do not treat these issues in the manner they are treated in scientific disciplines including economics. They contain broad and general principles and provide a basic framework. The details have to be worked out by people themselves in each age. But in their enthusiasm the Muslim economists occasionally try to read such meanings into the verses of the Qur'ān which are not there or which need not be searched for in the Qur'ān because they are common knowledge and are confirmed by casual observation. The point is that if a fact can be seen and confirmed by observation or reason there is hardly any reason to search for an evidence in the Qur'ān or the *Sunnah* which often has to be established by laboured interpretations. For example, there can hardly be a dispute that a well-looked-after worker would be more productive than a neglected worker. Some people have unnecessarily tried to drag in the Islamic texts such as Qur'ānic verses and traditions of the Prophet (peace be upon him) and have also resorted to a somewhat laboured interpretation relating to the slaves of the early Islamic era to prove this point.

A related point concerns the confusion which often takes place by not recognizing the distinction between 'Islamic' and 'Islamic framework'. By 'Islamic' we mean something sacred, something revealed by God or enjoined by the Prophet (peace be upon him). Whatever is 'Islamic' in this sense is immutable. But some people append the adjective 'Islamic' with the concepts propounded by human beings, such as Islamic profit, Islamic bank, Islamic business, etc. Sometimes the adjective Islamic is not appended but the discussion implies that the writer or the speaker intends to attach a sanctity to it. This needs to be clarified. All that is said within 'Islamic framework' need not be Islamic in the sense of having a permanent validity, since it is a product of human thought and is thus open to examination.

4.2 The Assumption of an Ideal Islamic Society

Most of the literature on Islamic economics assumes an ideal Islamic society which does not exist anywhere and the probability of its coming into being in the near future is also remote. Should the Muslim economists continue making this assumption? The assumption of an ideal Islamic society is an analytical tool which presents a relationship of dependence between the ideal and the actual phenomena. Theories stated in this framework explain how the two phenomena are interrelated and what are the factors which cause disturbance in this relationship. In this context it is a potent tool.

But the Muslim economists should realize that the ideal Islamic society is a special case within a large range of possibilities. The ideal Islamic society may continue to be an ideal to be achieved. But it is necessary that the concrete social reality of the actual Islamic society should be studied. This will help in shedding some of the romanticism in which many Muslim economists rejoice most of the time.

The idealism of Muslim economists has also done some harm to the scope of Islamic economics. Since the analysis is perceived in the context of ideal Islamic conditions, most of the ugly problems such as unemployment, inflation, trade cycles there is a tendency to assume that those problems would simply not be there. Since in an ideal Islamic economy those problems would not exist, the Muslim economists tend to feel that one need not even seriously 'study' them. In our view this is an overly simplistic approach. These problems are real life issues and there is no reason to believe that they would not arise in an ideal Islamic economy. It is possible that Muslims do not behave as expected even in an ideal society and this might lead to the rise of such problems. Therefore, Muslim economists should face the reality and discuss the problems of real life.

4.3 General Theory of Islamic Economy

Islamic economics is at times criticized on the ground that it has no general theory of an Islamic economy.[33] It is even dismissed as utopian and non-operational. Is this criticism fair? A general theory of economy can emerge from the study of real life conditions. The theory, as discussed earlier, is an abstraction of a complex reality. It is intended to explain, analyze and predict the behaviour of real life variables. But it is generally agreed that there does not exist an Islamic society anywhere in the world. How can a general theory be developed about a non-existent society? This is precisely the reason why Islamic economics at the present is scarcely able to articulate Islamic positions on economic issues.

In this situation it seems unfair to demand a general theory of Islamic economy. At best the Muslim economists may be expected to formulate a general theory of transition to Islamic economy. But a theory of transition is a complex matter because the economies of the world differ widely in their resource-endowment, value system and social infrastructure. As a result, there does not exist any generally accepted theory of change. Islamic movements in different countries have advocated different theses and there exists a wide controversy on the most suitable path to change. In our opinion, the evolution of a generally accepted route to Islamization would require concerted efforts of the scholars of different disciplines. What is the role of Muslim economists in this context? Should they sit back and wait for the opportune moment till a generally accepted theory of change emerges? In our opinion, Muslim economists have both the responsibility and the capacity to break the ice and take the necessary initiative.

We believe that a theory of transition to Islamic economy, much less the general theory of Islamic economy, cannot emerge from the level of discussion and the methodology of research in vogue. To set the stage for a theory of transition as a first step, considerable preliminary research will have to be done. A beginning can be made in the following direction. (Fig 2 below illustrates the points):

GENERAL THEORY OF ISLAMIC ECONOMY

Fig. 2

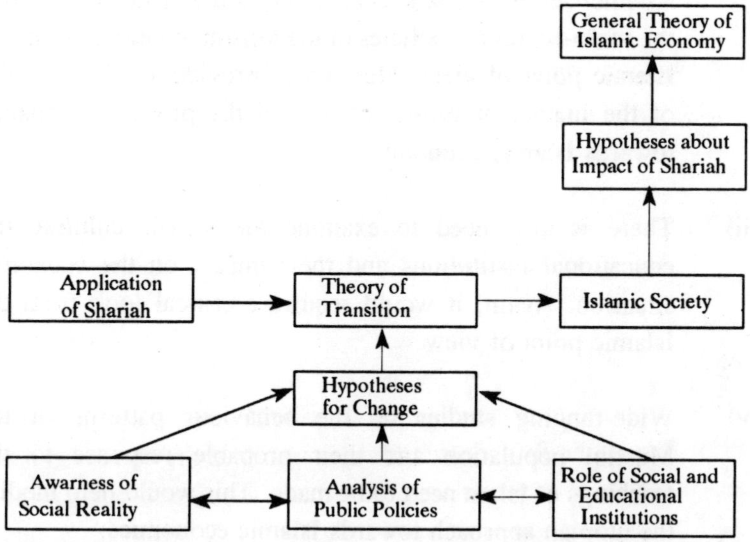

(i) Since the Muslim countries are expected to adopt Islamic economic precepts in preference, to other countries, they must initiate the process without loss of time. A beginning should be made by doing research on the real-life social and economic conditions of the Muslim countries. A series of research projects should be conceived on a master plan. The focus of these studies should be relationship between these conditions and the known phenomenon of non-adherence to Islam in actual practice. The development economists have done a lot of research on the real life conditions of the Third World including the Muslim countries. Their work, however, is both inadequate and, to some extent, irrelevant for the present purpose. It is inadequate because it is not related to the Islamic framework. Instead it has been related to the secular framework. It is also irrelevant because it has used the neoclassical economic tools which are often value-loaded and may not be suitable for the purpose. Therefore, such designs of research projects would have to be conceived which may lead to a better awareness of the real-life conditions of the Muslim countries.

(ii) Another series of research projects should critically examine the socio-economic policies of the Muslim countries from the Islamic point of view. This would provide a consciousness of the impact of those policies on the process of change towards Islamic economy.

(iii) There is also need to examine the social, cultural and educational institutions and their impact on the economic situation. Again, it would require a critical look from the Islamic point of view.

(iv) Wide-ranging studies on the behaviour patterns of the Muslim population and their probable response to the teachings of Islam need to be made. This would help modify the utopian approach towards Islamic economics.

Basic research organized on this pattern and conceived in a broad and coordinated plan would lead to a much better understanding of the existing situation. This research should not only be of a conceptual nature. It should also involve field work. Modern logistics and information technology should be fully utilized so as to help the researchers to bring to limelight actual conditions in which human beings, including Muslims, are living. A good awareness of the existing conditions is a must for developing any general theory of change. This awareness cannot come by mere conceptual exercises. The Muslim economists must go to the ground realities.

A generally acceptable *theory of transition* to Islamic economy is a pre-requisite to a *general theory of Islamic economy*. The general theory of Islamic economy would be an explanation and analysis of the Islamic economy as and when it comes into existence. To ask for a general theory of a non-existing economy is to demand the impossible. Attempts to produce such a theory cannot be more than an intellectual exercise on the part of Muslim scholars.

5. CONCLUDING REMARKS

In this era, the world at large and the Muslim *ummah* in particular, is suffering from a set of obstinate and insoluble economic problems such as unemployment, inflation, unequal distribution of income, poverty, balance of payments difficulties, burden of indebtedness and exploitation of the weak nations by the powerful ones. These problems present a serious challenge to Islamic economics. If Islamic economics can present plausible solutions to these problems, it would be accepted by the world, whatever its method of inquiry. Therefore, in the final analysis, it is not the method of inquiry that is important; it is the contribution that Islamic economics can make to economic progress and prosperity they matters. Islamic economics need not be confined to any one method. It should remain open to all the methods provided the inquiry remains within the basic framework of Islam and satisfies the twin criteria of reason and empirical validity.

Islamic economics is open to examination by Muslims and non-Muslims alike. It is ultimately the weight of its evidence and the rigour of its analysis that will establish its merit. Therefore, the Muslim economists should come out of the romanticism of the ideal Islamic society. They should devote greater attention to the analysis and solution of the present-day problems rather than keep recounting the bygone glory of Islam. This does not mean that Islamic economics should discard the historical perspective. It only means that historical data need be used to learn lessons for the present rather than to rejoice in the glory of the past.

The assumption of an ideal Islamic society should be kept as a goal to be achieved. The main occupation of the Muslim economists should, however, be to present an analysis of the application of the Islamic principles in the present-day society. It would not only generate a theory of transition which is missing at the present but is also likely to persuade the unconcerned spectator to think seriously about the Islamic economic system.

Four

ISLAMIC ECONOMICS IN PRACTICE

In this chapter we shall give a brief account of some Islamic economic institutions like Islamic banks, *zakāh*, insurance, *waqf* and *ḥisbah* as they exist today. While doing so we shall indicate the problems and challenges being faced by these institutions. The objective is to highlight the efforts made so far by the Muslims in translating Islamic economic ideas into reality and to predict the direction of their future development.

1. ISLAMIC BANKS

Perhaps in no other area has the practice of Islamic economics taken precedence over theory as in Islamic banking. Since Islam totally prohibits interest the mention of Islamisation of economy instantly turns one's mind to the experiments of establishing banks without interest.

The fifties and the sixties saw a number of theoretical studies for establishing interest-free banks.[1] But the actual implementation of Islamic banking had to wait until the mid-seventies when the Islamic Development Bank was established at Jeddah under the charter of the Organisation of Islamic Conference with the avowed objective of providing interest-free finance to Muslim countries.[2] Soon after that, a number of private Islamic banks were established in different countries of the world such as Egypt, Sudan, Kuwait, United Arab

Emirates, Malaysia, Cyprus, Luxembourg, Denmark. In the early eighties, two countries viz. Pakistan and Iran attempted to Islamise their entire banking system and prohibited all transactions explicitly involving interest on capital. In 1994 there were more than 200 Islamic banks in different parts of the world.[3]

The Islamic banks carry their business on the basis of equity-participation (*mushārakah,* and *muḍārabah*), leasing (*ijārah*), lease-purchase (*ijārah wa iqtinā'*), cost-plus financing, (*bay' murābaḥah*), and rent-sharing. These institutions have also innovated in devising some new financial instruments like Participatory Term Certificates (PTC), Term Finance Certificates (TFC), *Muqāraḍah* Bonds, Leasing Certificates, etc.

The Islamisation of banks in Pakistan and Iran seems to have survived the initial shock of change. Similarly, the private Islamic banks elsewhere are operating on profit. These banks have attracted large amounts of deposits and often have surplus liquidity.

The Islamic banks face a number of challenges. First, they have not as yet been successful in devising an interest-free mechanism to place their funds on a short-term basis. They face the same problem in financing consumer loans and government deficits. Second, the risk involved in profit-sharing seems to be so high that most of the banks have resorted to those techniques of financing which bring them a fixed assured return. As a result, there is a lot of genuine criticism that these banks have not abolished interest but have in fact only changed the nomenclature of their transactions.[4] Third, the Islamic banks do not have the legal support of central banks of their respective countries (except for Pakistan and Iran), which exposes them to great risks. Fourth, the Islamic banks do not have the necessary expertise and trained manpower to appraise, monitor, evaluate and audit the projects they are required to finance. As a result, they cannot expand despite having financial liquidity.

The future of the Islamic banks hinges, by and large, on their ability to find a viable alternative to interest for financing all types of loans. They should recognise that their success in abolishing interest has been at least partial and that they have yet to go a long way in their search for a satisfactory alternative to interest. Simultaneously, the Islamic banks need to improve their managerial capabilities by training their personnel in project appraisal, monitoring, evaluation and performance auditing. Moreover, the future of Islamic banks also depends on developing and putting into practice such accounting standards which provide timely and reliable information of the type that the Islamic banks would require for profit-sharing, rent-sharing or for cost-plus financing. There standards are yet to be developed. The Islamic banks would have to work hard to persuade their clients to accept these standards so that a reliable information base is established.

2. *ZAKĀH*

Zakāh is an obligatory financial levy on all surplus wealth and agricultural income of the Muslims. It is charged at varying rates and can be collected by the state. Its objective is to provide financial support to specified categories of people such as the poor and the needy. The institution of *zakāh* had existed in all Muslim societies throughout Muslim history but was neglected during the colonial rule. With the independence of Muslim states after the Second World War, the movement to rejuvenate this institution was started. Some countries like Bangladesh, Pakistan, Saudi Arabia, Sudan, Iran, Libya, UAE and Kuwait have passed formal legislation in that regard. In these countries the state or autonomous organisations collect and distribute *zakāh*.

Conceptually, *zakāh* is supposed to be a major instrument for providing social security, eradicating poverty, curbing excessive economic disparities, and stimulating economic activity by transferring substantial purchasing power to the have-nots. But in practice it has not played the role expected of it in any of the countries where *zakāh* has been introduced. The main reason has been the limited scale on which this institution has been allowed to operate. The governments of these countries have not allowed this institution the pivotal position it enjoys in the theoretical framework of Islam. Moreover, the management of *zakāh* leaves much to be desired. Idle *zakāh* balances, leakage of funds, inadequate coverage of *zakāh* assessees and lack of proper accounting, monitoring and evaluation are some of the problems being faced by these institutions.

Zakāh, nevertheless, has a bright future. Unlike the task of introducing an interest-free economic system, which is a highly difficult task since interest is deeply entrenched in the whole financial system, the efficient operation of the institution of *zakāh* is a much more manageable task. It does not need the demolition of the existing system. It only requires the establishment and strengthening of a new institution for which the Muslim masses show considerable enthusiasm. Therefore, the future of *zākāh* largely depends on the keenness with which the Muslim states establish and operate it.

3. INSURANCE

The contemporary insurance business has been widely criticised for its non-conformance with the Islamic principles.[5] It has been proposed that mutual insurance in which all policy holders stand to indemnify each others' loss would be nearer to the letter and spirit of Islam.[6]

Unfortunately, the Muslim states have not shown much enthusiasm to Islamise the insurance business. But some of the Islamic banks like Dār al-Māl al-Islāmī, Fayṣal Group of Islamic Banks, and the al-Barakah Group of Islamic Banks, etc., have set up Islamic solidarity companies which operate on Islamic principles. But so far their operations have not sufficiently expanded to create an impact in this sector.

The future of Islamic insurance depends on the interest shown by the Muslim states in amending their laws and bringing structural changes in the existing insurance business.

4. *WAQF*

The institution of *waqf* signifies a foundation set up by keeping a property in perpetual existence and making its income available for specified beneficiaries. This institution has been in existence from the very early days of Islam. It has always played an important social and economic role. The *waqf* properties have traditionally financed expenditure on mosques, schools, research, hospitals, social services and defence. Almost all Muslim countries have the institution of *waqf* in one form or the other.[7] This institution was developed in the Ottoman empire to a very significant degree so that very large tracts of arable land and other properties of significant value were owned by the *awqāf*.[8]

During the colonial rule, the Muslim lands saw enactment of secular laws and establishment of *awqāf* departments. At present almost every Muslim country has some form of *waqf* but its management has fallen into incompetent hands. Because of poor management and government interference the incentive to establish private *awqāf* has also weakened. However, lately the institution of *waqf* has shown a renewed vigour in some Muslim countries, of which perhaps the best example is Turkey where a large number of very useful and active *awqāf* have been established during the last two decades.

The Muslims need to reactivate this institution. As a first step, an inventory of existing *awqāf* in the Muslim countries should be made. It should be followed by taking appropriate legal, administrative and social measures to improve their management. The institution of *waqf* has a great potential and can be utilised to improve the education, research, health and defence capabilities of the Muslim states.

1.5 *AL-ḤISBAH*

The institution of *ḥisbah* has its roots in the early days of Islam when the Muslim states established a separate office to supervise markets, to provide municipal services, and to settle petty disputes.[9] Throughout Muslim history this institution has existed in one form or the other until the colonial governments handed over the functions performed by *ḥisbah* to various secular ministries.

Pakistan is perhaps the only Muslim country which has attempted to re-create this institution, albeit in a modified form. It has established an office of the *Muḥtasib* who has jurisdiction over the administrative excesses of the federal government departments and agencies. This institution provides protection to the ordinary citizens against administrative wrongs. Thus the office of the *Muḥtasib* in Pakistan has a limited role. It does not cover the provincial or local government departments and functionaries. It also does not protect a citizen against the malpractices of business firms. Despite these shortcomings, the institution has been widely acclaimed for its healthy role. There has been widespread demand to expand the scope and role of the *Muḥtasib* in the future.

Five

HOPE FOR THE FUTURE

1. INTRODUCTION

In this chapter we shall argue that Islamic economics provides a hope for the future. The profile of the future world economy can be conceived from its present state. If the present trends continue, the economic future of human beings on this globe does not hold much promise. Some of the economic problems, as mentioned earlier, are so obstinate that they have survived all conventional wisdom. As the 21st century draws nearer, these problems are likely to be aggravated. The present economic order, based on neoclassical ideas, is not likely to steer clear the human ship of these stormy waters. Because, firstly, neoclassical economics, being a positive discipline, does not play an active role in directing the human behaviour or economic events. It merely explains or rationalises them. Second, some of the basic postulates of neoclassical economics such as man's inherent selfishness, unregulated free enterprise, consumer sovereignty, absolute freedom to earn, save, invest or waste are instrumental in creating these problems. As we shall argue later, the solution of the present day economic problems requires a complete departure from the contemporary conventional wisdom. Our basic assertion is that Islamic economics holds the key to mankind's future economic problems. It approaches the economic problem of man from a completely new angle. A serious and objective study of Islamic economic principles has the potential of leading the present society into a more just and humane future.

The following discussion will examine some of the more serious problems of the contemporary society and will show the approach of Islamic economics to these problems. The objective is to show that the principles of Islamic economics gives hope to man whose future otherwise looks bleak. The pressure of future economic problems will force human beings to search for a more just and humane economic order. Perhaps at that time, Islamic economics will present a ray of hope.

2. ISLAMIC APPROACH TO CONTEMPORARY ECONOMIC PROBLEMS

2.1 Unemployment and Inflation

Since 1960s the economies of the free world have been facing the twin problems of inflation and unemployment. Earlier, it was believed that the two problems had an inverse relationship. If we were to control inflation, we would get higher unemployment, and *vice versa*. But the experience of the recent past has been particularly perplexing to economists. So far no recipe has succeeded. The formulas tried so far include the management of fiscal deficit, incomes policy, control of money supply, manipulation of exchange rates, supply side economic package, etc.

The problem has survived all attempts at its solution because none of the policies has struck at the root cause of the problem. The main cause of unemployment is interest on capital which retards the level of investment, leaving physical and human resources unemployed. At the going rate of interest there will always remain some investment proposals which will not be able to convince the potential investors that they would be able to earn enough to pay the interest. Therefore, some projects would be set aside as nonviable.

Thus, the solution of involuntary unemployment lies in reducing the rate of interest to zero.[1] The question as to how this can be done does not concern us at the moment. Perhaps, this can be left as a challenge to human ingenuity, once it is recognised that the root cause of unemployment is interest on finance and our first priority is to eradicate it.

Incidentally, Keynes also analysed this problem along these lines and recommended reduction of the rate of interest to its technical minimum. (He thought it to be 2% at that time). This he termed as the 'euthanasia of the rentier'. He prescribed deficit financing or expansionary spending after the rate of interest had been reduced to its technical minimum. Unfortunately, the Keynesian advice was not properly heeded. Its first part, which pertained to the reduction of the rate of interest to its technical minimum, was discarded and the policy of expansionary spending by way of Beveridge's social insurance package was adopted. The result was that, on the one hand, brakes on investment (in the form of interest) kept on being applied, and on the other, the accelerator of public spending on social insurance was continuously pressed. The economy started giving serious jerks. The unemployment caused by high rates of interest was obstinate. It simply refused to go down while inflation was striding as a result of deficit financing. The social security system visualised by the new welfare economics (and now deeply institutionalised) had left only two options before the governments: to raise funds through taxes or to borrow on interest. The first solution dampened the economy further. The second not only increased the fiscal deficit and thus inflation but also distributed income in favour of the rentier class and led to economic injustice.

The Islamic position is quite simple: abolish interest on capital in all its forms and allow the investment to rise to its maximum. It will increase employment levels, reducing the need for social security spending. Second, from an Islamic viewpoint deficit financing does not appear to be a desirable policy. The once golden rule of balanced budget is closer to the ethos of Islam.[2] Once this is accepted, the only problem and of course, a formidable one — would be to develop an institutional arrangement for providing interest-free finance. To our mind, human efforts should have been focused on this question instead of elaborating the rather easier course of providing social security benefits.

So far as the problem of inflation is concerned, the Islamic policy takes care of that also. First, one of the causes of inflation is interest itself, since the latter enters into the cost of production and thus becomes a part of the price of the products. This point might not have appeared plausible under the assumption of perfect competition. But now when we know that corporations wield enormous economic power and are almost autonomous in fixing the price of their products, it is accepted that interest enters into the price level and causes inflation.[3] Once we abolish interest, prices would come down to the extent the interest entered in the cost of production. Second, the abolition of interest would lead to higher investment and to greater supply of goods and services. This, too, will become an element in bringing down the price level. Third, *zakāh* is a tax on financial wealth and agricultural income and is collected and distributed at the local level to provide assistance to those who need it for one reason or the other. The community at the local level and the family at the micro level are responsible for looking after the poor and the indigent. The government only takes up the residual needs of the poor and that too through taxation and other revenues rather than through deficit financing. Fourth, Islam extols simple living which leads to a consumer behaviour sharply distinct from the consumerism prevalent in the Western society. Nor is this feasible in an environment where interest-bearing finance is not available. Islam also does not approve that people should live beyond their means. Thus the cultural pattern prescribed by Islam keeps the inflationary forces in check. Fifth, Islam visualizes an economy wherein the production sector is preferably organized on a profit-sharing basis so that labour has a stake in the well-being of the industry. As a result, the chances of wage-push inflation are reduced to a minimum.[4]

In brief, Islam follows a straightforward approach in tackling the twin problems of unemployment and inflation. The foremost measures are abolition of interest, balanced budget, effective collection and disbursement of *zakāh* and a consumer behaviour based on the values of Islam. The neoclassical approach to solve these problems is topsy turvy. It does not seek to abolish interest which is the main cause of unemployment. It tends, on the contrary, to have recourse to deficit financing to provide for social insurance and debt-servicing measures which generate inflation. Thus the said approach would lead the economy to disasters of the worst kind.

2.2 Economic development

2.2.1 Concept

Almost all the countries of the world profess their commitment to achieve economic development. This is obvious for the developing countries since they have a keen desire to catch up with the developed countries of the world. The developed countries also want to sustain their development, and would like to do so *ad infinitum*. With slight variation, the models for development being followed by the developing countries are those of the prosperous industrial countries. All the recipes for development are attempts to replicate the development processes of those countries. The objective is to increase the stock of physical goods and services for the population as a whole and thus a higher per capita share of goods and services.

The experience of over half a century of development, however, does not provide a very rosy picture. The income differentials between the poor countries and the rich countries are greater now than they were half a century ago. Despite all the efforts to increase capital formation, deepening of capital stock and industrialization and urbanization the developing countries are nowhere even near the Western models they are trying to follow.[5] The position in advanced countries is also no less worrisome. Amidst affluence there is poverty. Environment and ecology are under continuous threat. The waste of non-renewable resources, especially of energy, is depleting the reserves that would be available to posterity. The Western nations are worried about sustaining the present standards of living. With calls for a new international economic order the anxiety of the advanced countries has only increased as the known resources of the earth do not seem to be sufficient to allow a similar lifestyle for everyone. This fact has necessitated that a fresh look be cast on the conventional approaches to development.[6]

The Islamic concept of development is distinct from the conventional Western approach. First, the ultimate objective of human society is to achieve *falāḥ* and not merely material prosperity. Second, Islam emphasizes economic justice in distribution of income and wealth. If a society moves from state A to state B in such a manner that its distributional inequalities are reduced, in Islamic parlance it is development even though there might be no increase in the absolute size of the resources. Third, Islam conceives of a development philosophy which builds on the local cultural and social traditions, relies on local talent and physical resources, and involves the entire population of the area concerned in the process.

2.2.2 Strategy

Islam seeks to transform the society from its state of initial endowment to a state of *falāḥ*. Since the initial conditions differ from region to region, we shall take up two extreme cases to illustrate the development strategy of Islam. In the first case, let us imagine a poor country in sub-Sahara Africa or South Asia with dense population and a low level of income. The Islamic development strategy for this type of country will be to rely mainly on its own physical, human and technological resources. The development objective will be to achieve a state of *falāḥ*. The objective will be translated basically to fulfil the basic needs of the population with a degree of austerity. The development effort will concentrate on development of human resources, construction of necessary infrastructure like roads or ports, and development of appropriate technologies. As far as possible, local raw material and local talent will be used. This effort will be supplemented with a programme for the spiritual development of the people through persuasion, formal education, public policies, institutionalization of moral values. Welfare of the population will be conceived as an end by itself. There will be no ambition to introduce high technology. As far as possible, recourse will not be made to procurement of finance abroad except that which comes as donation or the loan made available on an interest-free basis. Public policy will be devoted to improving distribution of wealth and income, providing preferential treatment to those who are handicapped, and creating the conditions that would involve the common people in development activities. In such a country, per capita income might be far below what we find in some of the industrially advanced countries today. From an Islamic point of view, however, this country will be closer to the state of *falāḥ* and thus treated as developed.

The second case might be that of a rich country like some OPEC states. The development strategy for such countries will still have the same objective of achieving *falāḥ*. They will have a high stock of capital. They will focus on industrial development, introduction of high technology, providing a materially prosperous lifestyle for their people. But the overall considerations of economic justice, spiritual growth, participation of local population in decision-making, and developing local talent will remain the dominant considerations. Such countries can set aside some resources either by way of interest-free loans or grants to other countries or for the development of defence industries. Such countries will face the serious risk of drifting into a consumerist society of the Western kind. Therefore, a sizable chunk of resources should be spent by them on the spiritual training of the people through persuasion, formal education, sound and wholesome public policies, and institutionalization of the moral values of Islam. These measures will help material prosperity to become the means of promoting *falāḥ* rather than to a high consumption permissive society. From an Islamic point of view these countries will be closer to *falāḥ* and thus more developed than the countries following the model of the contemporary Western societies. (see Fig. 3)

Fig 3.

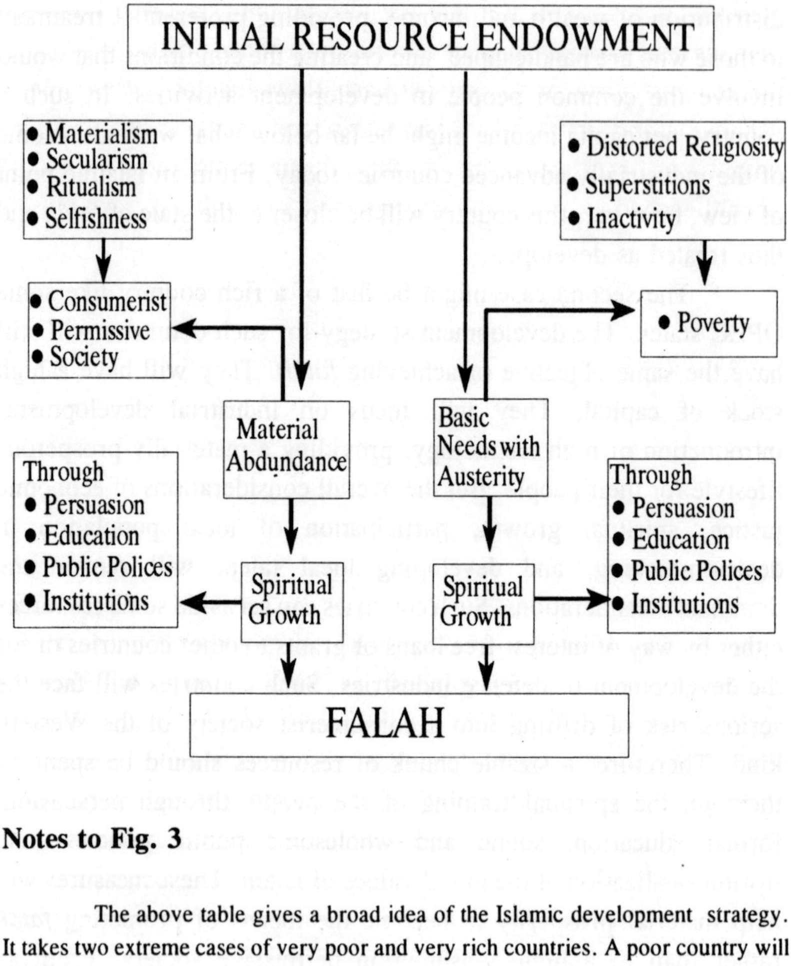

Notes to Fig. 3

The above table gives a broad idea of the Islamic development strategy. It takes two extreme cases of very poor and very rich countries. A poor country will achieve *falāḥ* if it tries to manage herself within its own means and promotes the spiritual growth of the people through persuasion, education and public policies (right-hand side). It will be considered 'developed' in the Islamic sense of the expression even though its GNP and per capita income might be nowhere near those of the developed countries. If such a country ignores the spiritual growth of its people, it would not be considered developed. It will be a 'poor' country in the Islamic sense of the expression.

Similarly, if we look at the left-hand side of the diagram, it shows the strategy for a resource-rich country. Such a country will be considered 'developed' in the Islamic sense only if it engages in the spiritual growth of its people in addition to concerning itself with material development. Otherwise it will be a materialistic economy like the one of the present-day Western countries.

2.2.3 Investment Criteria

The investment criteria in the Western economic models follow the famous economic efficiency criteria determined in the light of the benefit-cost ratio or discounted cash flow analysis. Although the technique appears to be value-neutral, certain value judgments are implicit in it. The validity of the criteria using these techniques would depend on whether a particular society upholds them as valid value judgments. But unfortunately the technique is being applied indiscriminately. Some of the value judgments implicit in the technique are as follows:

(i) A project with net higher benefit is preferable to a project with lower net benefit. This value judgment, on the face of it, appears to be quite reasonable. Yet in the real world it may not be so. We notice almost every day that politicians set aside the economic efficiency criteria and approve projects on purely political, ethnic, or regional considerations. As long as the politicians have the support of the people, their decisions cannot be termed as 'inefficient' — even on purely technical (i.e. economic) grounds. The basic assumption of economics is that each individual is the best judge of his own welfare and that the collective welfare of the people is optimized if they are left free to choose for themselves. Since the politicians decide on the basis of the wishes of the people in their locality, their decisions cannot be termed as irrational or 'inefficient' merely because they do not follow the economist's calculations.

(ii) The prevalent project evaluation techniques assume that the tastes and habits of the people would remain unchanged so that a project conceived to be most beneficial would continue to be so even after 10 or 15 years. This is an unreasonable assumption. We know that in a rapidly changing world which places a premium on innovation, tastes and habits undergo a change after some time. Thus a project considered to be beneficial today on the basis of cost-benefit analysis might subsequently turn out to be useless and even harmful in the years to come.

(iii) It ignores the equity consideration among different sets of people. The project appraised to be beneficial on the basis of highest net benefits may turn out to be socially undesirable since it may lead to transfer of resources from the poor to the rich.

(iv) The discounting technique ignores inter-generational equity. It assumes that the positive time preference is constant over time while the fact may be different. It is possible that the present value of a project's benefits is higher to the present generation in the case of, say, a fertilizer project which consumes natural gas as raw material. But it is conceivable that from the point of view of the future generations, the value of perceived benefits is much lower as it would deplete the natural gas reserves for them and would lead to genuine hardship. But the economic efficiency criteria is blind to such considerations.

(v) The discounted cash flow analysis is based on the concept of time value of money initially propounded by Bhom Bawerk. The theory is of doubtful validity in its application to project appraisal. Its anchor is the assertion that the people prefer present goods to future goods. This statement is true in the case of goods which one consumes in the present moment. But the future goods which exist only because one does not consume them right at the present moment and are thus represented by one's savings contradict the above assertion. In the case of savings, a person prefers future goods over present goods. That is why he does not consume them in the present moment. Thus, every penny that is being saved anywhere in lieu of that penny the saver has a negative time preference. Incidentally, the money that is being invested in a project is the money that has been saved by someone. Thus determining the present value of money by discounting it does not make any sense.[7]

Because of the above reservations about economic efficiency, the investment decisions in the Islamic framework follow the criteria of average profitability as modified in the light of social, political and cultural considerations. Detailed procedures can be worked out to translate this general principle in practice.

2.2.4 Development Planning

Contemporary development plans involve mechanical calculations relating to savings, capital formation, GNP, GAP, per capita income, development projects, infrastructure to be built, equipment to be imported, sources of finance to be tapped, taxes to be levied, and foreign assistance to be contracted, etc. These plans often do not give the slightest indication that they have anything to do with the human beings living in a country. What is totally missing from this picture is one on whom the whole attention ought to be focused — man.

As compared with this, the Islamic focus is on human beings. Man occupies the central position. A typical plan, in the Islamic framework, should adopt the following course. It should assess the human resource profile of the economy, lay down targets for nutrition, health, education, transport and communication, etc. These targets should then be translated into inputs required in terms of investment. The whole planning process should focus on the development of human beings. Man should occupy the central position. Priority should be accorded to training and education and research in science and technology. The educational system should ensure equal opportunities for all. The course contents and other teaching inputs should be brought to a uniform standard. Similarly, regional disparities should be reduced on a priority basis, especially the differences between the rural and urban sectors.

2.2.5 Foreign Aid

The contribution of foreign aid in the development of poor countries is of doubtful significance.[8] The need for foreign aid was originally propagated by the Western economists on the basis of the now famous theory of 'vicious circle'. There is ample evidence to show that the theory is of little validity. The fact that the industrially rich countries developed without foreign aid proves beyond doubt that the theory of vicious circle is not valid.[9] But the poor countries of the Third World are trapped in the web of foreign debt. The drain on their resources in the form of debt service and interest payments is so heavy that now there is a substantial outflow of resources from the poor countries to the rich countries.[10] The rich countries are playing the role of the rentier and aim at maximizing their benefits from the financial resources of the poor countries.

Foreign aid, in its actual operation, is a mechanism by which the donor countries stimulate their own economies rather than the economies of the recipient countries. Loans are provided to finance the projects which have a high priority for the donors. The stories of tied loans in which most of the money goes back to the creditor countries are too well known to be reproduced here.

The alarming situation of indebtedness of the Latin American and other poor countries has been created mainly by the profiteering of the financial institutions of the developed countries. This is eminently obvious from the fact that almost all financial institutions have set up 'development' or 'marketing' departments whose primary responsibility is to persuade the prospective clients to accept loans. These departments are manned by highly qualified people who first visit the Third World countries, persuade their elite about their latent credit needs, prepare projects for them, help them complete all the paper work, and in certain cases even indulge in malpractices to coax those countries into accepting loans. Once the loans are accepted, the concern of the creditors becomes mainly confined to receiving their pound of flesh rather than ensuring that the loans are well utilized by the recipient countries. In fact the amount loaned is often wasted, siphoned off to private coffers, or at least used ineffectively.

There is a great sense of alarm about the growing inability of the Third World countries to service their debts. Warnings are often issued about the imminent collapse of the world financial system. Economists of all shades and creeds have suggested solutions to remedy the situation.[11] In fact, the solutions are too many to be counted. But unfortunately none of the solutions is bold enough to effectively solve the debt problem.

The Islamic approach to the whole problem appears radical by the going standards and is likely to be effective in remedying the situation. To mention one of the most important features of that approach, it proposes the abolition of interest on all kinds of loans.[12] So, the first step in the Islamic strategy is that all interest payments should be written off and the creditors should get only the principal amounts and that too in easy instalments. This would immediately reduce the debt considerably.[13] For the future, no loan should be contracted on interest. Finance should flow to the needy countries, if it has to flow, only on the basis of profit-and-loss sharing or equity finance.

Obviously, this approach would not be very palatable for the rentier nations who also possess the military power to force the debtor countries to return the principal along with huge amounts of interest. But the problem of international debt will get from bad to worse if this major operation is postponed. The international community should get together to work out an arrangement which writes off all past interest and makes future financing either on the basis of interest-free loans or of profit-and-loss sharing. In fact, the real challenge for economics lies in this field. The economists of the world should accord the highest priority to research geared to suggesting institutional arrangements for interest-free financing.

2.3 Technology

The whole world is in the grip of a rapid technological revolution. The innovations in technology are affecting the social, cultural and economic relationships in a vast variety of ways. Since most of research and development is taking place in the private sector, there is little public control over it. Developments in technology have raised grave moral issues such as reckless use of laser technology in surgery, probabilities of the development of a monster in laboratories, marketing of insufficiently tested drugs and synthetic foods, invasion of privacy by the police, income tax and security agencies, use of weapons by criminals and terrorists, development of ABC weapons, etc.[14] On the economic front, every new wave of technological development has rendered some people unemployed, necessitating their retraining and creating the problem of structural unemployment.[15] In the international field, technology rents have been a significant source of transfer of resources from the poor to the rich countries. In 1980, for example, the developing countries paid about $ 2 billion by way of royalties and fees, mainly to the industrial countries.[16] Most of the technological development is taking place in the Western countries. For example, in 1980 the developing countries had only 6% of the total patent rights.[17] The patent rights of technology are a major barrier in the acquisition of new technologies by the developing countries.

From an Islamic point of view, there is little justification for an unplanned spread of technology. What would seem to conform with the Islamic ethos is the development of technology within the following framework:

(i) All new inventions should be assessed as to how they would affect the employment situation and to what extent it conforms to consideration of justice and equity. Before an invention is allowed to come into market, a comprehensive plan for the re-training and replacement of those who will be affected should be prepared.

(ii) As far as possible, new technology should be built on local talent and physical resources, and should be adapted to local needs. Uncritical acceptance of all new technologies, regardless of their suitability to the local conditions and their potential for social good or evil, should be discouraged.

(iii) Considerations of environmental protection and ecology should be kept in view while adopting every technological advancements.

(iv) Ethical guidelines should be issued for the use of technology in such fields as medicine, food, personnel management, etc.

(v) The Islamic framework visualizes cooperation at the international level. One of the tenets of Islam is that all knowledge should be shared. This obviously raises questions about the cost of developing new knowledge and the threat from parasitic free-riders. For these very problems international cooperation is required which not only prepares a framework for sharing the cost of technology development but also a plan for involving the developing countries in creating new knowledge. The myth of technology transfer has now almost exploded. Perhaps technology cannot be effectively transferred to the developing countries except at the cost of the developed countries losing their edge over the developing countries. This is not easy to come by. A more acceptable arrangement could be to involve the talent of the developing countries in the creation of new knowledge and new technologies suitable for their local environments. The developed countries can play a leading role in developing the talent of the poor countries.

2.4 Economic power

The classical and neoclassical economic models do not give due weight to the fact that economic power plays an important role in the real life. Economic power is a fact of life. People are born with unequal abilities and opportunities. As a result, some are likely to accumulate more economic power even though they are living within the legal framework and do not make any conscious effort to exploit others. Economic power provides the rich with the means for the suppression and exploitation of the weak. The classical assumption was that the economic power would not adversely affect the economic relationship since perfect competition would not let that happen. But the period after the Second World War has witnessed the emergence of global corporations. Capitalism has entered a new phase in its evolution. The national corporations have given way to the global corporations. These corporations are a conglomerate of economic power. They locate their operations where they can optimize their profits and market shares. They can evade national laws since they can move their operations very quickly to a more suitable location. The decisions of the global corporations affect the internal conditions of national governments. For example, if a corporation decides to disinvest from one country and move to another, that might adversely affect the employment and supply conditions of the former nation. Similarly, the global corporation have a system of pricing their products which allows them to reap exploitative profits. The outputs of plants in one country are shipped to another country where it has facilities for further processing. This output becomes raw material in the other location, where it is priced arbitrarily and often exorbitantly. The world has not been able to devise the mechanism to control and regulate the activities of the global corporations.

We notice a similar situation at the national and international levels. The corporations which operate at the national level and have some sort of monopoly or oligopoly in the market are not accountable to anyone for the misuse of their economic power. At the international level the economically powerful countries have the freedom and ability to behave irresponsibly and adopt policies which are harmful to other nations. This is not merely a hypothetical possibility. The tariff policies, exchange rate policies, and manipulation of commodity trade by the developed countries continuously operate against the interests of the developing countries. There is nothing that the weaker nations can do against these powerful nations.[18]

The Islamic perception is that the economy should be regulated in such a manner that economic power does not accumulate in a few hands. Islam recognizes inborn inequalities in human faculties with the result that some human beings have the ability to accumulate more economic power than others. At the micro level, Islam does not allow people to make unjustified earnings which are the major sources of concentration of economic power. Secondly, Islam attempts to distribute the economic power through a number of policies such as its inheritance laws, system of *zakāh* and public policies which attempt to reduce the inborn inequalities e.g. by providing equal educational opportunities, equal access to information, etc. But perhaps the greatest of all the measures against the concentration of economic power is the Islamic principle of accountability. It makes every individual, whether working for an organization or for the government, accountable for his actions.[19]

In the case of global corporations, for example, the Islamic system would not, in the first instance, permit the emergence of powerful economic giants. The source of this economic power lies in three important features of capitalism: availability of capital on interest, the principle of limited liability, and the organization of production on the basis of wage-labour. The interested reader may refer to Appendices I and II for a brief discussion of the subject. Suffice to say here that these three features of capitalism allow the corporations to collect huge amounts of finance without incurring a proportionate degree of risk. They are able to earn super profits by having the ability to control the markets and fix the prices. The Islamic system does not allow credit on interest. It also does not seem to approve the principle of limited liability. Moreover, it leans towards encouraging organization of production in such a manner that workers become partners rather than mere wage-earners. In this way, it considerably widens the base of wealth. The possibility of the global corporation to emerge in the Islamic system is thus considerably minimized. The Islamic ethos seems to encourage an economy that would be dominated by a large number of small or medium size firms which compete and cooperate with one another.

But if despite all this, large corporations do emerge within the national boundaries of a country, or beyond them, the Islamic system of accountability comes into play. At the national level it will suggest a revision of the scope of traditional auditing so that the management of corporations is held accountable for its actions and omissions. At the international level the Islamic framework would support the establishment of a Supreme Audit Institution of the World which should be responsible to audit the accounts of the global corporations. The scope of this institution should be to hold managers of these corporations accountable for their various decisions regarding output, pricing, investment, quality of products, environmental effects, etc. The same institution should also be responsible for auditing the policies of the national governments which affect other nations.

At this stage, this might look like a wild idea. But it is quite in conformity with the contemporary thinking which is supportive of the idea of accountability for public managers. If public managers are to be held accountable for their actions, why not also private managers? Similarly, the scope of accountability need not remain restricted to now famous three Es — economy, efficiency, effectiveness. It can also encompass at least two more E's—ethics and environment. It is unfortunate that despite all the lip service paid to universal human rights, to freedom, liberty and equality, the world has not given any serious thought to the accountability of the economically powerful so that the freedom of the weak is protected.

2.5 Consumer sovereignty

2.5.1 Consumerism

The mainstream economics assumes — that the consumer is sovereign. But the rise of corporate power has reduced the assumption to a myth. The corporations can produce and market almost anything they like with the help of advertisement campaigns which have become an art in themselves. The sales promotion techniques employ the most ingenious methods to persuade the consumer what is good for him. In fact the whole economy is geared not just to satisfying but also to creating demand. Finance also comes to the help of the corporate sector. Consumers are offered all sorts of facilities to enable them to spend recklessly. The present-day consumerist society promotes the pursuit of acquiring more and more goods. The consumer is allured into the purchase of new models, latest designs and 'modern fashions' in almost all goods although he might already possesses them. Some of these changed models might possess some new elements and also improved features but perhaps one could do without them if one so chose. But the advertising campaigns build so much pressure on the individual's nerves that one feels helpless and rushes to get the new model. This is a situation which has virtually eroded the sovereignty of the consumer. The consumers are psychologically forced to buy a countless number of things which they do not need nor have time to enjoy. These resources could have been utilized elsewhere in more productive channels.

It seems that the time has come when it is almost impossible to change the advertisement culture because media and finance — the two most powerful institutions — have also developed a vested interest in the perpetuation of the consumerist society. The Islamic framework simply revolts against reckless consumerism. It promotes simple living. It encourages moderation. But it also does not curtail the freedom of the business to advertise its products except that it can broadly regulate it so as to make it free from cheating or gross mis-statements.

In these circumstances, we think that the Islamic teachings of simple living can be institutionalised by attacking the problem from another angle. We should educate the people in consumption skills. At present the entire educational system is geared to the teaching of production skills. People do not get any training in consumption skills — identifying the method to select the best buy, the best time of purchase, the method to use various goods to obtain maximum value out of them; to develop the skill of everyday maintenance of household assets, to acquire the capacity to order quantity levels that are economical, economic purchase outlets, etc. This type of training should be part of the regular education of the students so that by the time when they graduate they are 'mature' consumers with a reduced tendency to be waylaid by advertisements or marketing campaigns.

Another method to protect the consumer from the market onslaught is to provide him more information on various aspects of life. The neoclassical economists consider information about prices as adequate. But this has become inadequate due to the complexities of life. It is also important, at present, to know how things are being produced, and in which quantities, and at what cost? What is their effect on the environment? What is their effect on human health? How far are the 'advertised' facts true? How far are the 'claims' of the producers correct?

This work is being done at a rudimentary level in the industrially advanced countries by media reports. But this is inadequate on two grounds: first, the media people are not technically trained to analyze, test and vouchsafe all types of information. Therefore, they cannot go deep enough into the information. Second, the media has a vested interest in not offending the corporate sector which supports the media by advertisement revenues. Therefore, we need independent institutions responsible for the collection, analysis and dissemination of valid, relevant and sufficient information. These institutions should be like our observatories for space research. We should also have 'observatories' for social and economic information research. These institutions must be independent of the government. Preferably, they should be attached to universities. They should be supported by powerful computers. They should protect the consumer against misinformation and misreporting.

2.6 Role of public policy

Neoclassical economics relies on public policies such as tax and tariff incentives, subsidies, foreign exchange quotas, etc., to bring about an economic change. This strategy presupposes that the individuals will respond to these public policies in the goal-adequate direction. They do not provide for any mechanism to ensure that the individuals do, in fact, act in that fashion. As a result, the government has no means to ensure a satisfactory response. It cannot even precisely 'predict' the outcome of a public policy. An example will suffice. It is not sufficient for a government to give tax rebates for stimulating investments unless businessmen perceive it profitable to make investment or until the total environment is congenial to do so. It is necessary, therefore, that the government should also engage in an educational campaign to elicit goal-adequate behaviour from the people. These controls should comprise widespread information to increase the knowledge of individuals about the future or campaigns designed to persuade people to adopt the appropriate patterns of behaviour. For instance, in the above example, the tax rebates could be accompanied by widely-publicized campaigns about the government's intention to undertake investment if the private response is inadequate. Such a campaign could be an instrument to elicit the goal-adequate response from the public. Since the neoclassical economics does not concern itself with changing the human behaviour, it also does not provide for such 'controls' to make the public policies a success.

Although such techniques are in vogue in some European countries, the mainstream economics has not yet recognised them and has not formulated methods to induce people towards the desirable pattern of behaviour. The field of these controls is very wide. However, these controls have to remain within the overall framework of freedom and human dignity.

Seen in this perspective, Islamic economics has an edge over the mainstream economics. Islamic economics does not only study the behaviour of individuals, it also aims at changing human behaviour in the goal-adequate direction. The job of the Muslim economist is not only to observe and predict but also to propose public policies designed to motivate people and to persuade them to reform their behaviour. Most of the Muslim economists talk of an educational process to bring about this change with a provision to invoke the coercive apparatus of the state for ensuring the goal-adequate behaviour. It is unfortunate that the Muslim economists have not gone beyond this point. But the difference between the mainstream economics and Islamic economics is that while the former does not recognize it as a legitimate field of inquiry[20] the latter considers it a vital component of its subject matter.

Thus we can see that Islamic economics holds a promise which the traditional economics does not. In the final analysis if the knowledge of economics does not help in ushering in a goal-adequate social environment it is nothing more than an intellectual luxury of the economists.

3. CONCLUDING REMARKS

In this chapter we have outlined the basic concepts of Islamic economics. We have argued that Islamic economics has the potential to solve some of the serious economic problems and that this potential would lead the world to benefit from it in the future.

Islamic economics, however, has not as yet developed a theoretical body of doctrine. Most of what is written consists of general principles and that too in the framework of an ideal Islamic economy which, incidentally, does not exist anywhere in the world. Only a few of its ideas have found a place in the real world partly because its potential is not widely known. It is time that the Muslim economists come out of their shell and start addressing humanity at large. They need not concern themselves with the Islamic economy alone. Their immediate concern should be to show the world that Islamic economics can present acceptable solutions to the economic problems of the contemporary world as such. They need to make a formidable case for Islamic economics. Islamic economics has the potential to persuade the economists of the world because, firstly, all the tenets of Islamic economics are rational and in this age rational arguments are readily acceptable. Secondly, there is a lot of dissatisfaction among professional economists about the assumptions, analytical framework and conclusions of the neoclassical economics. They are already looking for an alternate paradigm. In this situation Islamic economics can provide a ray of hope.

The Muslim economists need to change their focus. Instead of developing a theory in the framework of an ideal Islamic society, they should choose a contemporary economy and show, on the basis of real life data, that the primary cause of the existing economic problems lies in deviation from the Islamic principles of economic management.

The economics that can grow with valid assumptions, adequate methodology and has a body of economic theory capable of ushering in a humane society would be the economics of the future. Islamic economics has the potential of meeting this challenge. The only requirement for the Muslim economists is to present their case in a persuasive manner.

The time seems to have come when the basic postulates of Islamic economics will be accepted by the world as *the economics*. The present economics will wither away or get assimilated into Islamic economics. It is possible, however, that due to bias against religion the title of Islamic economics might not be readily accepted. Even while the appellation 'Islamic' might be distasteful for people, there is little doubt that with the passage of time the content of Islamic economics will be welcomed by a large section of humanity who will look up to it as a source of hope and relief.

Six

DIRECTION OF FUTURE RESEARCH

The purpose of the present chapter is to indicate some of the future research priorities for economics. The main conclusion is that the overall framework of Islamic economics can contribute to the development of economics in a direction which will make this discipline meaningful and suitable for the challenges of the future. In fact, our prediction is that the real life problems of the future would virtually force the Islamic solutions on humanity. But it may take much longer for humanity to reach these solutions in a hit and miss fashion. Islamic economics can expedite the process of discovery of those solutions which are essentially needed by humanity. The only precondition is that the world should shrug off its preconceived notions and prejudices against religion and religion-related ideas. After all, the civilized world owes most of its wisdom to religious sources. Even the success of the capitalist system is attributed to Christian ethics. In the following discussion we shall point out some of the most urgent research tasks in order to bring it closer to the Islamic approach to economics.

1. HOLISTIC APPROACH

If economics has to play a helpful role in directing the human future, it must perceive the actual relationship that has emerged between the household, the market, the government, the environment and the international institutions. It must conceive humanity not merely as an economic but also as a social, political and psychological entity whose survival and quality of life depend on all the above factors and their interdependence.

Economists should not be content with raising such questions as: Is the firm profitable? Is there full employment? Are prices stable? Is the growth rate satisfactory? Instead, they should also ask questions regarding human, psychological, motivational and environmental needs. They should also see in which way the economy is deviating from the path of human *falāḥ*. For concentrating on the economic problem of man is too narrow an approach. It reduces human beings to merely economic creatures, which does offence to both human nature and personality. In fact, there are no economic problems as such! There are only *human* problems. They should be perceived by keeping the human beings in the centre. For example, the relevant questions regarding technology are: How does it affect the employment of those already in jobs? How will it prevent those who are seeking jobs so as to enter the labour market? Who will pay for the re-training and rehabilitation of those misplaced? How will the new technology affect the quality of life of those who will work under the new conditions? What type of stress and strain will it bring? How will the new technology affect the international market? How will it affect the international relations? What will be the new tariff system and how will it affect the existing agreements with other nations? Scores of such questions will merit discussion.

The traditional economics has treated most of such questions as exogenous.[1] One of the reasons for the reluctance to accept this approach is that it introduces qualitative variables into the theory, which violates the economists' obsession with numbers and quantities. Their eagerness to transform everything into quantitative analysis so that some analytical technique comes handy dissuades them from adopting this approach. In fact, one of the reasons economics could not become a realistic social science is that it has tried to grapple with complex human problems as merely economic problems. As a result, it has lost the comprehensiveness of a human science.

Islamic economics takes a comprehensive view of the human problems. It employs a multi-disciplinary approach to these problems. This is an area where Islamic economics can make a contribution to the global pool of knowledge.

2. SEARCH FOR AN INTEREST-FREE INTERNATIONAL ECONOMIC ORDER

One of the greatest challenges for the twenty-first century would be to develop the vision of an alternative economic order which is free from interest on capital. Islamic economics has produced a body of knowledge which attempts to show how financial institutions can be established on an interest-free basis. But there are still a number of unresolved questions. Such a system would truly succeed if the world as a whole agrees to abolish interest. This would mean 'euthanasia of the rentier' — individuals, organizations, and states. This is an imminent task before humanity if it has to unshackle man from the bonds of finance.

Human development has accepted the political freedom of man as a valid concept but it has not yet fully recognized the importance of the economic freedom of man as a desirable goal. The economic freedom of man will never be realized so far as the fruits of one's labour are allowed to be reaped by the rentier in the form of interest. The challenge before the economists of the world is to find out an institutional mechanism which provides finance free of interest so that the idle resources of the world are used for the benefit of humanity. So far the economists have given very little thought to this great challenge. The day humanity is able to abolish interest effectively will be the day of its real emancipation. Political freedom is only a half-way house. The abolition of interest would mean what Keynes has rightly termed as a 'sea change'. The foremost item on the future research agenda should be to find out a viable and suitable interest-free international economic order.

3. TECHNOLOGY

Economists have not given adequate attention to the subject of technology. The technological revolution has engulfed the entire world. The information technology is influencing our lifestyles, production patterns, resource allocation and development priorities. Economists should not be mute spectators, allowing things to happen as they do. They must analyze the impact of technology on human lives. In this area Islamic economics has a contribution to make. It raises such questions as stated below:

> What are the implications of technology for economic justice, both positive and negative? This means, how is technology going to affect the relative shares of different sectors of the economy in the national pie? Or, how can technology be used to reduce economic and infrastructural disparities between rural and urban and backward and developed regions, and between the rich and poor nations?
>
> What could be the international mechanism to share the fruits of human intellectual endeavor without creating the 'free-rider' problem?
>
> What are the possible ethical implications of the new technology and how can it be harnessed to the benefit of humanity?
>
> What are the technological research priorities for the world and for the different nations?

These and similar questions should be the priority of the economists during the years to come.

4. ECONOMIC POWER

Another area which has received scant attention of the economists is the question of economic power. Islamic economics accords a central position to economic justice. The whole question of economic justice hinges on the basic question: how does society protect its weak from its strong? The same is true at the international level. How does the world organize itself to protect the weak nations from the tyranny of the strong in the field of economics? It would require an analysis of the actual conditions to show the various forms of misuse of power against the weak. Then it would require the formulation of such public policies or the development of such institutions as would protect the weak from the strong. Laws alone would not help. Power has to be controlled. It must be made accountable by making individuals participate in decision-making. The Islamic concepts of *khilāfah* (vicegerency), *shūrā* (consultation), *ukhūwah* (brotherhood), *'adl* (justice), *iḥsān* (benevolence) have the potential of making a contribution to tackle the problem of economic power.

APPENDIX I

LIABILITY OF THE SHAREHOLDERS

Some Muslim scholars have argued that the liability of the shareholders in a joint stock economy in the Islamic framework is limited to the extent of their own capital or by guarantee. Their argument goes like this: There is no doubt that the sum borrowed by someone must be paid back. (This is evident from the emphasis that the Prophet (peace be upon him) attached to the repayment of loans inasmuch as he would refuse to pray on the dead body of a companion if the latter owed a debt, and he himself would arrange its repayment before performing the prayer). But in the case of a joint stock company, the shareholders are not the borrowers. Instead, the company, as a 'legal person' is the borrower. Therefore, the liability of the company is unlimited. It must repay its debt by selling all its assets. However, the liability of the shareholders remains limited to the extent of their share in the capital assets of the company.

In brief, the whole issue boils down to the question: can we accept the concept of 'incorporation' as Islamic? The usual reply is that there is evidence in the primary sources of Islam which shows recognition of legal persons. Some examples of legal person are *bayt al-māl* (public treasury), mosque, *awqāf*, etc. Therefore, a company can also be considered a legal person. This provides a mechanism for continuity in business and enables a large number of people to join hands without having to re-structure the business at the entry or exit of a shareholder.

Impressive as this line of argument might seem, it has certain weaknesses. First, even if we were to acknowledge that incorporation is lawful in Islam, it does not automatically follow that we can incorporate business entities. The evidence is regarding public offices which did not deal in commercial activities, especially the borrowing and lending of money. We shall have to search for a more explicit evidence in the primary sources of Islam to prove that incorporated entities could enter into a relationship of borrowing and lending as well. Second, the whole argument does not follow the logic of its reasoning. For example, if the actual borrower is the company and not the shareholders, then the liability of the shareholders should be nil. Why, then, should the shareholders have even a limited liability? Moreover, the basic question is: Who owns the assets of the company? The company itself or the shareholders? Suppose a company is liquidated, who will appropriate the realised sum? Of course, the shareholders will get the net realised sum, whether it is more or less than their own capital. If that is so, then, how can the shareholders escape the liability of the company's debts, if it is more than their own capital? Third, the entitlement of the shareholders to the profits of the company is unlimited. Whatever the company earns is the property of the shareholders. How, then, can we say that if the company suffers a loss, the liability of the shareholders will be limited only to their own capital?

If we were to accept the principle of unlimited liability, it will make the shareholders existing on a particular date liable for the debts of a company and those shareholders who had sold their shares and received profits in the past would go scot-free, although losses may have been caused by the wrong policies of those very shareholders who had sold their shares. Looked at from the Islamic viewpoint the whole mechanism of doing business with borrowed funds is alien to the spirit of Islam. Islam does not recognise interest on loans. It allows only interest-free loans. In all probability under an Islamic economic system, this type of funding will not be available in large quantities since people will not like to give their money to others on an interest-free basis so that the latter may invest it and earn a profit. Interest-free loans are encouraged to help needy people to meet their everyday needs. For business purposes, if someone needs additional finance, he should get it on a profit-and-loss sharing basis, thus risking his capital. If someone has any surplus capital, in all probability, he would like to earn a return on it rather than to give it someone else on an interest-free basis so that the latter may earn a return. Therefore, very little interest-free credit is likely to be available in the Islamic economy. Also, this credit will most probably be in the form of day-to-day trade credit for short periods. For medium and long term finance some mechanism of profit-and-loss sharing will have to be introduced in the Islamic economy.

In our view, if capital is available only as equity, the question of limited liability of shareholders becomes irrelevant. The liability of shareholders emerges as an issue only where large sums of money (much larger than the capital of the company) are obtained on the promise to pay interest. Then, as a result of over-trading or careless management, if the company is unable to repay its debts, the shareholder's personal wealth is provided an immunity. But this whole question is a non-issue in an Islamic economy. However, if in extremely rare situations a company does accumulate large trade debts or is unable to collect its own debts and goes bankrupt, the shareholders on whose behalf the company ran the business must be held liable for the repayment of the debts. To provide a legal basis for such a policy, the shareholders of the company should be asked explicitly to allow the management to borrow the money on an interest-free basis or to incur trade debts or to sell its products on credit. If the shareholders allow, then they should also be held responsible for the consequences of their decision.

The only thorny problem that remains is that of the shareholders who have left the company. One answer could be that the reserves of the company, which consist of its past profits, remain with the company, even when a certain shareholder leaves. Therefore, the existing shareholders who own those past profits as well, should accept the liability for the past debts as well. But, to our mind, this is only a theoretical possibility. In the absence of interest-bearing loans, the question of liability of shareholders will not be a major issue in the Islamic economy.

APPENDIX II

DISCOUNTING FOR PROJECT EVALUATION

The discounted cash flow (DCF) related techniques for project evaluation have their origin in the theory of interest developed by Eugene von Bhom Bawerk, an Austrian economist, in 1884.

Von Bhom Bawerk critically examined the then prevalent theories relating to the justification of interest on borrowed capital. He refuted all those theories, one by one, on rational grounds and concluded that none of them provided an adequate basis to justify interest on capital. After having done so, he raised the question: what, then, is the justification of interest on capital? It was in response to this question that he presented his theory of the time value of money. He argued that the utility of the present goods was more to an individual than the utility of future goods. Therefore, when X borrowed some money from Y, and promised to return it after one year, the utility of this money for X after one year would be less than its value for him in the present. Therefore, to compensate X for the reduction in value of the money, Y should pay some extra money (known as interest) to X. In this way, the value of money received by X after one year would be equal to the present value of this money for him.

Thus he derived the concept of the present value of money which was the value of money at the present moment. He postulated that the present value of all future streams of money can be worked out by discounting the future values for the number of years involved to the present (i.e. year zero). Thus discounting of future values to the present involved the reverse process of compounding of interest.

The concept of time value of money has been widely adopted by the economists. It is being used to appraise capital expenditure proposals by most of the financial institutions and development planning agencies of the world. It is also being taught in most of the universities and business schools as the basis for investment appraisal. The wide acceptance of the concept speaks for unquestioned reliance on interest as a tool for allocation of resources.

But the concept has not been seriously examined. The assertion that the present value of money is higher than the future value is true only in limited situations. If the question is about resources to be acquired, everyone will like to prefer them to have them sooner than later, because the value of those resources is higher in the present than in the future. But if the question concerns the consumption of resources, the present value of the resources could be higher or less than their future value. If it is higher, then an individual will like to consume those resources at the present moment of time. But if the future value is higher than the present, then he would like to save the resources for the future. Therefore, every act of saving, anywhere in the world, is a conclusive evidence of the fact that to the extent of the money saved the future value is higher than the present value. And the money being invested in a project is precisely that which was saved in the past since its future value was higher than the present value. Therefore, the basis for discounting is not sound on rational grounds.

The concept of discounting implicitly integrates certain other subjective and unrealistic assumptions. For example, it converts this preference to acquire resources now rather than in the future into a certain rate of discount. How is that rate determined? Implicitly, it is the rate of interest which would be paid to obtain the funds for investment or the expected rate of interest which can be earned on the benefits received. But with what logic do we convert our preference to acquire resources now rather than in the future into a certain rate of discount? How do we know that this preference is equal to a certain percentage?

The only reality is that a person of ordinary prudence prefers to acquire resources in the present rather than in the future. But by no logic does it lead us to convert this preference into a certain rate of discount. The question arises: How, then, would an entrepreneur decide between different alternatives in a situation like the one given below?

Suppose the initial investment in each case = $ 50,000.

Net Cash Inflows

Life of Project: 4 years

	Project A	Project B	Project C
1st year	$ 30,000	$ 16,250	$ 5,000
2nd year	$ 20,000	$ 16,250	$ 10,000
3rd year	$ 10,000	$ 20,000	$ 20,000
4th year	$ 5,000	$ 30,000	$ 30,000
	$ 65,000	$ 65,000	$ 65,000

The answer is that since an ordinary entrepreneur prefers to *acquire* resources earlier than later in time, he would prefer project A to B and project B to C. This can be said without any discounting. An examination of the cash flows leads us to this common sense answer.

It leads to a further question. What will be the decision if the cash flows are as follow:

Net Cash Inflows

Life of Project 4 years

	Project A	Project B	Project C
1st year	$ 30,000	$ 16,250	$ 5,000
2nd year	$ 20,000	$ 16,250	$ 10,000
3rd year	$ 10,000	$ 20,000	$ 20,000
4th year	$ 5,000	$ 30,000	$ 35,000
	$ 65,000	$ 65,000	$ 70,000

In such a situation the entrepreneur is in a fix. If he prefers project A to C, he would suffer an obvious loss of $ 5000. Should he forego these $ 5000 and choose project A which brings in higher cash flows in early periods? A simple answer is that he will look at the average rate of return on capital. In project A it is 32.5% per annum and in project C it is 35%. He will choose project C. But the supporters of the discounted cash flow techniques argue that he would choose project A if he discounts the cash flows at 10% as illustrated below :

Year	Present Value Factor for 10%		Present Value of Cash Inflows	
1st year	0.909	$ 27,270	$ 16,250	$ 4,545
2nd year	0.826	$ 16,250	x 3,170	$ 8,260
3rd year	0.751	$ 7,510		$ 15,020
4th year	0.683	$ 3,415		$ 23,905
Total		54,715	51,513	$ 51,730
Initial Investment		$ 50,000	$ 50,000	$ 50,000
N.P.V.		$ 4,715	$ 1,513	$ 1,730

Therefore, they argue that the average rate of return leads to the selection of an 'inefficient' project. But this argument implies that the criterion to select a project is the present value of cash flows, therefore, other decisions would be compared in the light of this criterion to determine their plausibility. But what is the logic of accepting the present value as the criterion for selection? It may be argued that the reason lies in the concept of positive time preference which assumes that the resources received earlier in time have a greater opportunity of being reinvested than the resources acquired later in time. But how do we know that they have the possibility of earning a certain percentage of return in the future (i.e. the rate of discount)?

It can be argued further that discounting is necessary since different cash flows have different levels of uncertainty. In the above sample it is possible that project A's cash flows have a higher certainty than those of project C. But this reasoning does not tell how can we convert 'uncertainty' into a certain rate of discount except that we do it arbitrarily. Moreover, even on this logic the practice differs from theory. In practice the same discount rate is applied to all projects and to all cash flows (inflows as well as outflows), whereas if we accept the logic of the above argument we should apply different rates to different projects and also different rates to cash inflows and cash outflows (according to their respective uncertainty). In practice this logic is not followed.

A question still remains to be answered: how shall we decide between two projects with different life cycles? A simple answer, again, is: by the average rate of return on capital. But what if the gestation period of the project with a higher yield is also longer than the gestation period of the project with a lower yield? The answer is that it is in conformity with everyday phenomenon. Even Robinson Crusoe had to accept a longer gestation period for a higher return. The question remains: how much increase in the rate of return would a businessmen want to accept an year's increase in the gestation period? For example, suppose in project A, the rate of return is 15%, and the gestation period is 4 years, and in project B the rate of return is 10%, but the gestation period is 3 years. Should the businessman accept another year's gestation period for an increase of 5% in the rate of return? We can talk of the question in the following manner. Suppose he chooses project A, what would he lose? He would lose 10% on project B which he could earn after 3 years. But he would be compensated in the long run by a higher return over the life of the project i.e. 15%. Therefore, as long as the rate of return on the shorter gestation period project remains lower than the rate of return on the longer gestation period he would continue to prefer the longer gestation period project. This further means that the real criterion is the expected average profit on a project over its life cycle and not the gestation period or timing of cash flows. It is only when the average rate of return on two projects is equal that the question of timing of cash flows comes in. In such a situation, a rational person would prefer a project which brings in higher cash flows sooner in its life cycle.

NOTES AND REFERENCES

ONE

1. For an excellent exposition, see I.R. al-Faruqi, *Tawḥīd: Its Implications for Thought and Life,* Washington D.C.: the International Institute of Islamic Thought, 1982.
2. Qur'ān (3:14), (14:3).
3. M. Asad, *The Message of the Qur'ān*: Gibraltar: Dar al-Andalus, 1980, p. 973 (commentary on verse 103:6).
4. Based on Caliph 'Umar b. al-Khaṭṭāb's understanding of verse 59:9 of the Qur'ān as reported by Abū Yūsuf, *Kitāb al-Kharāj* (Urdu translation) Lahore: Islamic Publications, 1966, p. 158.
5. Qur'ān (7:31), (17:70), etc.
6. Prophet Muḥammad's address on his last pilgrimage as reported by Muslim, *al-Jāmi' al-Sahīh, "Kitāb al-Īmān"*, tradition no. 259.
7. Qur'ān (6:141), etc.
8. "Each year 6 million hectares of productive land turns into worthless desert .... More than 11 million hectares of forests are destroyed yearly .... A leak from pesticide factory in Bhopal (India) killed more than 2000 people and blinded and injured over 200,000. Chernobyle nuclear reactor explosion sent nuclear fallout across Europe, increasing the risk of future human cancer .... During 1984-87, an estimated 60 million people died of diarrhoeal diseases related to unsafe drinking water and malnutrition". (*Our Common Future, Report of the World Commission on Environment and Development,* Oxford: Oxford University Press, 1987, pp. 2-3).
9. Qur'ān (18:46).
10. For an excellent exposition see T. Hazledine, *Full Employment without Inflation*, London: Macmillan, 1984, p. 264.

11. For a comprehensive treatment of the subject see A.S. Eichner, *Towards a New Economics*, London: Macmillan, 1986, pp. 10 ff.
12. For example, calculations made recently in West Germany show that dividing all households into 10 groups of 2.5 million in order of household wealth, the net effect of interest payments is a significant transfer of wealth to the two richest groups from the rest. (Margaret Kennedy, *Interest and Inflation-Free Money*, Permaculture Institute Publications, Steyerberg, Germany, 1988)
13. J. Robertson, *Future Wealth*, London, Cassell, 1989, p. 89
14. See Appendix-I
15. Qur'ān (2:275-277).
16. Ibn Mājah, *Sunan, "al-Tijārāt"*, chapt. 20 as quoted in M. Akram Khan, *Economic Teachings of Prophet Muhammad*, Islamabad: International Institute of Islamic Economics, 1989 *hadīth* (6:1).
17. M. Akram Khan, *Economic Teachings of Prophet Muhammad*, op. cit.; see *ḥadīth* (5:1-5).
18. S.R. Khan, *Profit-Loss-Sharing*, Karachi: Oxford University Press, 1987, p. 165, as quoted from Abraham Udovitch, *Partnership and Profit in Medieval Islam*, New Jersey: Princeton University Press, 1970, p. 184.
19. J. Roberston, op. cit. pp. 3-4.
20. This has been argued by A.A. Mawdudi, *Islam and Other Economic Systems* (Urdu), Lahore: Islamic Publications, 1960.
21. Juridical maxim no. 87 in *Majallah Ahkām al-'Adliyyah*, (Urdu), Lahore: Awqāf Department, 1981, p. 36.
22. *World Development Report 1992*, Washington: The World Bank, 1993, p. 278.
23. *Our Common Future*, op. cit., p. 69.
24. R.L. Kitchen, *Finance for the Developing Countries*, New York: John Wiley, 1988, p. 270.
25. M. Stewart, *Controlling the Economic Future*, Sussex: Wheatsheaf Books, 1983, p. 49. See also Alvin Tofler, *Powershift*, London: Bantam Books, 1991, p. 58.
26. *Our Common Future*, op. cit., p. 6.
27. J. Robertson, op. cit. , p. 76.
28. K.F. Flexner, *The Enlightened Society*, Lexington: Lexington Books, 1989, p. 78.
29. M. Akram Khan, *Economic Teachings of Prophet Muhammad*, op. cit.; see *ḥadīth* (9:1; 9:4).
30. T. Congdon, *The Debt Threat*, Oxford: Basil Blackwell, 1987.
31. T. Scitovsky, *Human Desire and Economic Satisfaction*, New York: Wheatsheaf Harvester, 1986, pp. 117 ff.
32. J. Robertson, op. cit., p. 2.

33. Hashmat Ali', *The Theory of Income Distribution under the Islamic Law*. Unpublished Ph.D. thesis, Georgetown University, Washington, D.C., 1953.
34. The Islamic injunctions against extravagance and waste (*isrāf* and *tabdhīr*) support this assertion.
35. *Word Development Report*, 1990. Washington D.C.: World Bank, 1990.
36. *Our Common Future*, op. cit., p. 6.
37. Edgar Owens, *The Future of Freedom in the Developing World*, New York: Pergamon Press, 1987, pp. 17-19.
38. J. Robertson, op. cit., p. 76.
39. For a detailed exposition, see E. Owens, op. cit.
40. Ibid.
41. This assertion is based on the understanding that man, being viceregent of God, is the focal point of the entire creation of God. It is he who should be the focus of all development effort.
42. This is based on the Islamic norms of cooperation *(ta'āwūn)* and consultation (*shūrā*).
43. A.A. Mawdudi, *Islam and Birth Control* (Urdu), Lahore: Islamic Publications, 1960.
44. For a detailed treatment, see M. Akram Khan, *Organising Zakāh*, Lahore: All Pakistan Islamic Education Congress, 1990.
45. *Our Common Future*, op. cit., p. 88.
46. This assertion is based on the Qur'ānic condemnation of niggardliness (*shuḥḥ*) and miserliness (*bukhl*). In our view, these traits of character would apply, by extension, to concealment of knowledge as well.

TWO

1. A number of bibliographies have appeared showing the amount of literature that has been produced on Islamic economics. See, e.g. the present writer's *Islamic Economics: Annotated Sources in English and Urdu*, (2 Vols.) Leicester: The Islamic Foundation, 1983, 1991; Tariqullah, *Islamic Economics: A Bibliography*, Jeddah: IRTI, 1984; Nienhaus, V., *Literature on Islamic Economics in English and German*, Koln: al-Kitab, Verlag, 1982. A quarterly publication of the Islamic Foundation entitled '*Index of Islamic Literature*' enlists the current literature on Islamic economics in each issue of the journal. *Index Islamicus* also presents a list of works on Islamic economics. *Islamic Periodica* from Malaysia publishes information on Islamic Economics as well.
2. If a date has to be placed on it, it is 1976 when over 200 Muslim intellectuals and economists gathered in Makkah to hold the first

International Conference on Islamic Economics. Since then, there has been a great deal of intellectual activity in this field.

3. For an excellent treatment of the subject see Baqai, Moin, "Societal Framework for Economic Development" in Haq and Baqai, *Employment, Distribution and Basic Needs in Pakistan*, Lahore: Progressive Publishers, 1986, pp. 371-407.
4. See, for example, World Commission on Development, *Our Common Future*, op. cit., p. 69.
5. K. Ahmad, "Problems of Research in Islamic Economics", in Aidit Ghazali and Syed Omar, (eds.), *Readings in the Concept and Methodology of Islamic Economics*, Selangor (Malaysia): Pelanduk Publications, 1989, pp. 141-154.
6. See H. Mintjes, *Social Justice in Islam,* Amsterdam: Institute for the Study of Religion, Free University, 1977.
7. These doubts were expressed by Volker Nienhaus in a personal letter to the present writer.
8. Q.V. "*Falah*" in Rāghib al-Isfahāni, *al-Mufradāt fi Gharīb al-Qur'ān*, Karachi: Noor Mohammad, Kārkhanah-i Tijārat-i Kutub, n.d.
9. Qur'ān (23:1).
10. Qur'ān (2:189), (3:130), (3:200), (5:35), (5:100).
11. Qur'ān (7:69), (8:45), (62:10).
12. Qur'ān (24:31), (28:67).
13. Qur'ān (87:14), (91:9).
14. Qur'ān (2:3), (64:16).
15. Qur'ān (2:219).
16. Maḥmūd 'Ālūsī, *Rūḥ-al-Ma'ānī*, vol.I, p.119, (verse 2:5).
17. Muslim, *al-Ṣaḥīḥ*, chap., "*Faḍā'il al-Ṣaḥābah*", *ḥadīth* 67.
18. Qur'ān (23:4).
19. Qur'ān (3:130).
20. Muftī M. Shafī', *"Ribā"* in *Urdu Encyclopaedia of Islam*, Lahore: Punjab University.
21. Qur'ān (23:8).
22. For instance, Abdullah Yusuf Ali and Maḥmūd 'Ālūsī, two important commentators of the Qur'ān, have made this point while explaining the verse (23:8).
23. Qur'ān (6:21), (6:135), (12:23), (28:37).
24. Qur'ān (6:21), (10:17), (10:69), (16:116).
25. Qur'ān (10:77), (20:69).
26. Qur'ān (5:90).
27. Qur'ān (23:6).
28. Qur'ān (5:90).
29. Qur'ān (23:4), (87:14), (91:9).
30. For example, Abdullah Yusuf Ali, op. cit. n.22 supra.

31. Qur'ān (3:104).
32. Qur'ān (23:3).
33. Qur'ān (5:35).
34. Qur'ān (41:10)
35. Qur'ān (4:1).
36. Qur'ān (49:10) and Muslim, op. cit. *"al-Birr wa al-Ṣilah"*, *ḥadīth* 80.
37. Qur'ān (5:2).
38. Muslim, op. cit., *al-Luqṭah*, *ḥadīth* 19.
39. Qur'ān., *Faḍā'il al-Ṣaḥābah*, *ḥadīth* 231.
40. Ibid., *"al-Zakāh" ḥadīth* 39-40.
41. For an anthology of the *Ḥadīth* literature on Islamic economics, see the present writer's *Economic Teachings of Prophet Muhammad* (Peace be upon him), op. cit.

THREE

1. Some of the works which give a comprehensive view of the methodological debate are: Mark Blaug, *The Methodology of Economics* (Cambridge: Cambridge University Press, 1980), Bruce Caldwell, *Appraisal and Criticism in Economics* (Boston: Allen and Unwin, 1984); Sheilla C. Dow, *Macro Economic Thought: A Methodological Approach* (Oxford: Basil Blackwell, 1985); A.S. Eichner, *Why Economics is not yet a Science*? (London:Macmillan, 1983); Daniel M. Hausman, *The Philosophy of Economics: An Anthology* (Cambridge: Cambridge University Press, 1984); J.J. Klant, *The Rules of the Game* (Cambridge: Cambridge University Press, 1984); and Peter Wiles and Guy Routh, *Economics in Disarray* (Oxford: Basil Blackwell, 1984).
2. M. Blaug (1980), op. cit., p. ix.
3. J.J. Klant, op. cit., p. 2.
4. Qur'ān (2:1).
5. Qur'ān (10:36), (53:28).
6. M.N. Siddiqi, (1982), p. 18.
7. All the injunctions in the Qur'ān and *Ḥadīth* with regard to caring sharing and generosity others are a testimony to this statement.
8. Qur'ān (59:9).
9. Anwar Iqbal Qureshi, *The Fiscal System of Islam*, Lahore: Institute of Islamic Culture, 1978.
10. *The Economist*, London, 23 August, 1986, p. 75.
11. This is based on such Qur'ānic verses (6:32), (14:3), (16:107), (75:20-21), (100:8).
12. The Qur'ān categorically expresses its disapproval of monasticism. See (57:27).

13. The Prophet (peace be upon him) said: "(Lawful) wealth for a virtuous man is an excellent thing". See al-Ḥākim,*al-Mustadrak,* vol.II, *hadīth* no.1, Hyderabad (India): Dā'irah al-Ma'ārif al-Nizāmiyyah, 1340 A.H.
14. Qur'ān 4:11.
15. Sir John Hicks has observed: "There is much of economic theory which is pursued for no better reason than its intellectual attraction; it is a good game". (J.R. Hicks, *Causality in Economics*, Oxford: Basil Blackwell, 1979, p.viii). See also T. Hutchison "Our Methodological Crises" in Peter Wiles and G. Routh, *Economics in Disarray,* Oxford: Basil Blackwell, 1984, pp. 1-21.
16. Translation of the Qur'ānic verses has been taken from Ahmad Ali, *Qur'ān: A Contemporary Translation,* Karachi: Arkash Publishing, 1984.
17. For a persuasive discussion on the subject, see Abū A.H. Sulaymān, "Islamization of Knowledge with special reference to Political Science", *The American Journal of Islamic Social Sciences,* (2:2), December 1985, pp. 263-290.
18. Garudy, R. "The Balance Sheet of Western Philosophy", *AJISS* Herndon, VA., (2:2), pp. 169-178.
19. One of the prayers of the Prophet (peace be upon him) bears testimony to the fact that he was very keen for the rational explanation of natural phenomenon. He used to pray: 'God! Grant me knowledge of the ultimate nature of things; *Allāhumma arinā haqā'iq al-ashyā' kamā hiya,* a well known tradition quoted in Sufi works such as 'Alī b. 'Uthmān al-Hajwīrī (d. 465/1072) *Kashf al-Mahjūb*, p.166, as referred to by Saeed Sheikh in his notes on Iqbal's *Reconstruction of Religious Thought in Islam* (Lahore: Institute of Islamic Culture, 1986), p. 158.
20. Iqbal, M. *Reconstruction of Religious Thought in Islam*, op. cit., p. 100.
21. Qur'ān, (2:164), (15:16), (16:68-69), (21:33), (24:43-44), (30:48), (35:9), (36:40), (37:6), (41:12), (45:5), (50:6), (67:5), (85:1).
22. Qur'ān (2:260).
23. Qur'ān (6:75-78).
24. Qur'ān (16:68), (20:38), (28:7).
25. Hutchison, T., op. cit., p. 5.
26. Qur'ān e.g. (31:34).
27. T. Hutchison, op. cit., p. 5.
28. We find certain verses in the Qur'ān which bear witness to both the traits of human nature. For example, the Qur'ān says: "Selfishness is ever present in human souls" (4:128). At another place it says: "We created man of finest possibilities" (95:4).

29. Qur'ān (7:188).
30. Qur'ān (20:71), (20:131), (28:60), (87:17).
31. M.N. Siddiqi, *Recent Works on the History of Islamic Economic Thought*, (research paper), Jeddah: Centre for Research in Islamic Economics, 1980.
32. For a brief account of various paradigms in economics, see M. Ariff, "Towards the Sharī'ah Paradigm of Islamic Economics: The Beginning of a Scientific Revolution", *.AJISS*, Herndon, VA., (2:1), 1985, pp. 79-99.
33. For example, Nienhaus, V., "Islamic Economics — Policy between Pragmatism and Uopia", *Economics*, Tūbingen, (vol. 25) 1982, pp. 80-100.

FOUR

1. The most influential study is M.N. Siddiqi, *Banking Without Interest*, Leicester: The Islamic Foundation, 1983.
2. S.A. Meenai, *Islamic Development Bank*, London: Kegan Paul International, 1989.
3. For a comprehensive survey upto 1988 see John R. Presley, (ed.), *Directory of Islamic Financial Institutions,* London: Croom-Helm, 1988.
4. M. Akram Khan, "A Survey of Critical Literature on Interest-free Banking", *Journal of Islamic Banking and Finance*, Karachi (6:1), January 1989.
5. See, e.g, M. Muslehuddin, *Law of Insurance and Islam,* Lahore: Islamic Publications, 1969.
6. Ibid.
7. For a survey see Basar, Hasmet (ed.), *Management and Development of Awqaf Properties*, Jeddah: Islamic Research and Training Institute, 1989.
8. Barnes, J.R., *An Introduction to Religious Foundations in the Ottoman Empire*, Leiden: E.J. Brill, 1986.
9. Ibn Tamiyah, *Public Duties in Islam*, Leicester: The Islamic Foundation, 1981.

FIVE

1. Some people assert that Islam does not prescribe zero rate of interest, since in the case of Profit and Loss Sharing transactions also the capital suppliers get a return. Thus there is a positive cost of the capital. In fact, this interpretation of the position is based on the

capitalistic concept of 'capital' and 'interest'. In the capitalist framework, the creditors provide capital on interest. For the enterprise, this capital has a cost. The capital suppliers are distinct from the business entity. The business entity borrows capital at a cost. In this framework, some accounting theorists treat the capital of the shareholders as a liability of the business and the dividend paid as the 'cost of owners' capital'. But if we were to look rationally at this situation, it would be evident that the business firm is not a separate entity from the owners. The owners of the business supply capital (and some labour). For them, the profit of the business is not the 'cost' of the capital but a 'return' on it. In the Islamic framework, the capital joins as partner and owner. Therefore, the dividend on it is not the 'cost' of the capital. The concept of zero rate of interest remains valid in the Islamic framework since business firms do not borrow money on interest. The capital from the outsode joins as a partner and remains there as joint owner of the business. The share of profit on this capital is, thus, a return on capital and not its cost.

2. This is based on the Qur'ānic prescription of moderation (*iqtiṣād*) which is applicable to the public sector as well. See Qur'ān (17:29).

3. Kurt F.Flexner, *The Enlightened Society: The Economy with a Human Face*, Lexington, D.C. Heath & Co., 1989, p. 78.

4. M. Akram Khan, "Inflation and the Islamic Economy: A Closed Economy Model", in M. Ariff (ed.), *Monetary and Fiscal Economics of Islam*, Jeddah: ICRIE, 1982.

5. *World Commission on Development, Our Common Future*, Oxford: Oxford University Press, 1987 p. 6.

6. Qur'ān.

7. For an effective rebuttal of this concept see S.M. Ahmad, *Towards Interest-free Banking*, Lahore: Institute of Islamic Culture, 1989.

8. Arshad Zaman, *Dimensions of Self-Reliance and National Development*, Lahore: Pakistan Institute of National Affairs, 1989, p. 5.

9. P.T. Bauer, *Dissent on Development,* London: Weidenfield and Nicholson, 1976, p. 69.

10. For example, in 1985, the net transfer from the poor to the rich countries was $ 30 billion. See *Our Common Crisis*, op. cit., p. 69.

11. For a survey of proposals see Richard L. Kitchen, *Finance for the Developing Countries*, New York: John Wiley, 1988, pp. 307 ff.

12. Qur'ān, 2:275-77.

13. Kitchen, op.cit., p. 27.

14. E.J. Mishan, *Economic Myths and the Mythology of Economics*, Sussex: Wheatsheaf Books, 1986, pp. 131 ff.

15. Moinuddin Baqai, "Societal Framework for Economic Development", in Mahbubul Haq and Mouinuddin Baqai, *Employment, Distribution and Basic Needs in Pakistan*, Lahore: Progressive Publishers, 1986, pp. 371 - 407.
16. *Our Common Future*, op. cit., p. 87.
17. Our Common Future, op. cit., P. 82.
18. Qur'ān.
19. This is based on belief in the Day of Judgement. Traditions of the Prophet (peace be upon him) also specifically mention that each person is accountable. The same principle was extended to the affairs of this world by Muslims throughout their history.
20. Lowe, A., *Essays in Political Economics*, Sussex: Wheatsheaf Books, 1987.

SIX

1. Rostow, W.W., *Rich Countries and Poor Countries*, London: Westview Press, 1987, p. 13.

NOTES TO APPENDIX-I

1. Qur'ān (2:233), (28:27), (43:32).
2. Qur'ān (24:33).
3. Muslim, *al-Jāmī' al-Ṣaḥīḥ*, *al-Aymān*, *ḥadīth* 60.
4. A prominent discussion of this point is available in M. 'Umar Chapra, *The Economic System of Islam,* London: The Islamic Cultural Centre, 1970.
5. 'Alī b. Abī Bakr Al-Marghinānī, *al-Hīdāyāh*, *"Kitāb al-Ijārāt"*, vol. 3, Cairo: Muṣṭafā al-Bābī, n.d. p. 231.
6. Ibid.
7. Abū Dāwūd, *Sunan*, *"al-Kharāj wa al-Amārah wa al-Fay'"*.

GLOSSARY OF TERMS

'Adl. lit., justice. Refers to the principle enjoined by Islam and which is required to embrace the entire gamut of socio-economic relationships.

Aḥādīth. Plural of *ḥadīth*, (q.v. *ḥadīth* below).

Fay'. Originally used for the resources that the Muslim army took into possession from the enemy without having to enage in actual fighting. Subsequently, it came to be equated with all civil revenues except *zakāh*.

Ḥadīth (pl, *aḥādīth*). Record of the sayings, deeds or tacit approvals of the Prophet (peace be upon him).

Ḥalāl. Permitted by Islam.

Ḥarām. Prohibited by Islam.

Iḥsān. Lit., benevolence. Refers to a cluster of moral values such as spending on others, caring for neighbours and relatives, sacrifice for others, including all acts of altruistic character.

Iḥtikār. Withholding stocks from the market with a view to create scarcity and binding up prices artificially.

Iqtiṣād. Lit., saving; economy. Refers to moderation in behaviour, especially a middle road attitude between extravagance and miserliness.

Isrāf. Lit., to exceed the limits. Refers to reckless spending or spending on unlawful objects or living beyond means.

Mudārabah. A mode of business where two or more persons participate: one with capital and the other (or others) with labour and enterprise. The financier shares the profit with the entrepreneur according to mutually agreed terms. In the case of loss, it is borne by the financier alone.

Mushārakah. A mode of business in which more than one person join with capital and labour on the basis of profit-and-loss sharing.

Ribā. Lit., increment. Refers to a pre-determined increase on the amount loaned which increases over time. It is equivalent to interest.

Ribā al-fadl. An increase arising out of an unequal barter exchange of the same commodity with deferred delivery from one party.

Sharī'ah. Refers to divine guidance as given by the Qur'ān and the *Sunnah* and embodies all aspects of the Islamic faith including beliefs and practices.

Shirkah. See *Mushārakah*

Sunnah. Refers to the normative behaviour of the Prophet (peace be upon him) as evidenced by his utterances, and his tacit approvals.

Shūrā. Consultation.

Ta'āwun. Lit., cooperation. Refers to the God's command to cooperate in all acts of "goodness and piety".

Taqwā. Lit., piety; it is an essential trait of the character of a Muslim. It encompasses a number of values such as honesty, thankfulness to God, remembering God, justice, benevolence, spending in the way of God, etc.

Tabdhīr. Refers to wasting resources or spending them on unlawful objects.

Ummah. Refers to the Muslim community irrespective of colour, race, language or nationality.

Waqf. Charitable endowment. Appropriations or tying up of a property in perpetuity so that no proprietary rights can be exercised over the corpus but only over the usufruct.

Zakāh. The amount payable by a Muslim on his net wealth as a part of his religious obligation, mainly for the benefit of the poor and the needy. It is levied at the rate of 2.5 per cent on all financial assets and stock-in-trade of business; at the rate of 10% on agricultural produce of rain-irrigated cultivation and at 5% on the produce of artificially irrigated cultivation. It is payable at different rates on livestock reared for sale. The exemption limits are quite low, so that it has a very wide coverage.

Zulm. Refers to all forms of inequity, injustice and exploitation.

SELECTED BIBLIOGRAPHY

Nature of Islamic Economics

ARIFF, M., "Towards a Definition of Islamic Economics: Some Scientific Considerations", *JRIE,* Jeddah, (2:2), Winter 1985, pp. 87-103.

______, "The Islamisation of Knowledge and Some Methodological Issues in Paradigm-Building", *AJISS,* Washington, (4 : 1), September 1987, pp. 51-71.

CHOUDHURY, M.A., "Policy-Theoretical Foundations of Ethico-Economics", *Humanomics,* Cape Breton, (IV:3-4), 1988, pp. 1-7.

______, "Towards a Definition of Islamic Economic Theory and Development", *Contemporary Review,* London, August, 1981, pp. 76-82.

FARUQI, I. RAJI, AL-, "Islamising the Social Sciences", *al-Nahda,* Malaysia, (2:2), 1982.

KHAN, TARIQULLAH, *Islamic Economics: A Bibliography,* Jeddah: IRTI, 1984, pp. 156.

MANNAN, M.A., *Why is Islamic Economics Important? Seven Reasons for Believing,* Jeddah: ICRIE, 1982, pp. 26.

NIENHAUS, V., "Islamic Economics — Policy between Pragmatism and Utopia", *Economics,* Tubingen, (25), 1982, pp. 80-100.

______, "Restatement of Normative Economics: Western Approaches and Islamic Perspective", *Humanomics,* Cape Breton, (IV:3-4), 1988, pp. 27-65.

______, *Literature on Islamic Economics in English and German,* Koln: Al-Kitab Verlag, 1982, pp. 150.

______, "Monetary, Social and International Economics: Some Thoughts on the Islamic View", *Economics,* Tubingen, (28), 1983, pp. 71-91.

WEISS, DIETER, "Towards an Islamic Economy", *Economics,* Tubingen, (33), 1986, pp. 21-37.

Micro and Macro Economics

ANWAR, M., *Modelling Interest-Free Economy,* Herndon, VA: International Institute of Islamic Thought, 1987, pp. 120.

ARIFF, M., "Towards Establishing the Microfoundations of Islamic Economics: The Basis of the Basics", *The Islamic Quarterly,* London, (28:2), 1984, pp. 61-72.

ASHKER, AHMAD A., AL-, *On the Islamic Theory of Consumer Behavior: An Empirical Study in a Non-Islamic Country,* Durham: Centre for Middle Eastern and Islamic Studies, 1985, pp. 18.

CHOUDHURY, M.A., "The Micro-Economic Foundations of Islamic Economics: A Study in Social Economics", *AJISS,* Washington, (3:2), December 1986, pp. 231-245.

HASAN, ZUBAIR, "Theory of Profit: the Islamic Viewpoint", *JRIE,* Jeddah, (1:1), 1983, pp. 1-16.

______, *Macro Consumption Function in an Islamic Framework", JRIE,* Jeddah, (2:2), Winter 1985, pp. 79-81.

JARHI, M.ALI, AL-, "Towards an Islamic Macro Model of Distribution", *JRIE,* Jeddah, (2:2), Winter 1985, pp. 1-30.

KHAN, M. AKRAM, "Islamic Economics: The State of the Art" in *Challenge of Islamic Economics,* Lahore: All Pakistan Islamic Education Congress, 1986, pp. 31.

MANNAN, M.A., *Islamic Perspectives on Market Prices and Allocation,* Jeddah: International Centre for Research in Islamic Economics, 1982, pp. 30.

______, *The Frontiers of Islamic Economics,* Kuala Lumpur, July 1984, pp. 31.

NIENHAUS, V., "Epistemology, Methodology and Economic Policy : Some Thoughts on Mainstream", *Humanomics,* Cape Breton, (1:2), 1985, pp. 10-38.

Early Economic History of Islam

HASAN-UZ-ZAMAN, S.M., *The Economic Functions of the Early Islamic State,* Karachi: International Islamic Publishers. pp. 407.

HERSHLAG, Z.Y., *Introduction to the Modern Economic History of the Middle East,* Leiden: E.J.Brill, 1980, pp. 431

UDOVITCH, A.L., "The Constitution of the Traditional Islamic Marketplace" in S.N.Eisensradt, (ed.), *Patterns of Modernity,* London: Frances Pinter, 1987, pp. 150-171.

Economic System of Islam

AWAN, AKHTAR A., *Equality, Efficiency and Property Ownership in the Islamic Economic System,* London: University Press of America, 1983, pp. 111.

GHAUSSY, A. GHANIE, "Attempt at Defining an Islamic Economic Order", *Economics,* Tubingen, (37), 1988, pp. 9-39.

______, "The Islamic Economic Ethic and Economics", *Economics,* Tubingen, (31), 1985, pp. 71-96.

ISHAQUE, K.M., *Islamic Principles of Economic Management,* Karachi: Economic Research Unit, 1982, pp. 57.

KURAN, TiMUR, "The Economic System in Contemporary Islamic Thought: Interpretation and Assessment", *IJMES,* 1986, pp. 135-163.

MANNAN, M.A., *The Making of Islamic Economic Society: Islamic Dimensions in Economic Analysis,* Cairo: International Association of Islam Banks, 1984, pp. 535

NAQVI, S.N.H., *Individual Freedom, Social Welfare and Islamic Economic Order,* Islamabad: Pakistan Institute of Development Economics, 1981, pp. 40.

NASR, S.V.R., "Whither Islamic Economics? "*Islamic Quarterly,* London, (4), 1986, pp. 211-20.

RA'UF, M.A., *A Muslim's Reflections on Democratic Capitalism,* Washington D.C.: American Enterprise Institute for Public Policy Research, 1984, pp. 75.

SARDAR, Z., *Islamic Futures: The Shape of Ideas to Come,* London: Mansell Publishing, 1985, pp. 360.

TALEGHANI, S.M., *Society and Economics in Islam,* tr., R. Campbell, Berkeley: Mizan Press, 1982, pp. 230.

ZAIM, SABAHADDIN, "Islamic Economics as a System based on Human Values" in M. Ali, *Islamic Banks and Strategies for Economic Cooperation,* London: New Century Publishers, 1982, pp. 15-25.

Economic Growth and Development

CHISTI, SALIM, "Relative Stability of Interest-free Economy", *JRIE,* Jeddah, (3:1), 1985, pp. 3-12.

HASAN-UZ-ZAMAN, S.M., "Indexation - An Islamic Evaluation", *JRIE,* Jeddah, (2:2), Winter 1985, pp. 31-54.

KHAN, M. AKRAM, "Economic Growth and Development in Islam", *The Search,* (6), Winter 1985, pp. 142-166.

______, "Resource Allocation in Islamic Economy", *Islamic Quarterly,* London, (29:4), 1985, pp. 240-250.

MIRAKHOR, A., and ZAIDI, IQBAL, *Stabilization and Growth in an Open Islamic Economy* (typescript), 1987, pp. 36.

MANNAN, M.A., *Allocative Efficiency, Decision and Welfare Criteria in an Interest-free Islamic Economy,* London: The Muslim Institute for Research and Planning, 1980, pp. 32.

SIDDIQI, M. N., *An Islamic Approach to Economic Development,* London: The Muslim Institute for Research and Planning, June 1979, pp. 8.

ZARQA, M. ANAS, "Capital Allocation, Efficiency and Growth in an Interest-free Islamic Economy", *Journal of Economics and Administration,* Jeddah, (16), Nov 1982, pp. 43-55.

Monetary and Fiscal Economics

ARIFF, M. (ed), *Monetary and Fiscal Economics of Islam,* Jeddah: ICRIE, 1982, pp. 412.

______, "Islamic Banking: A Southeast Asian Perspective" in *Islamic Banking in Southeast Asia,* Singapore: ISEAS, 1988, pp. 194-212.

AHMAD, SHAIKH MAHMUD, *Towards Interest-free Banking,* Lahore: Institute of Islamic Culture, 1989, pp. 147.

AHMAD, ZIAUDDIN, IQBAL, MUNAWAR, and KHAN, M.F., *Money and Banking in Islam,* Islamabad: Institute of Policy Studies, 1983, pp. 300.

______, "Profitability of Islamic PLS Banks Comparing with Interest Banks", *JRIE,* Jeddah, (1:1), Summer 1983, pp. 66-68.

______, *Some Misgivings about Islamic Interest-free Banking,* Khartoum: Faysal Islamic Bank, 1985, pp. 23.

______, *Prohibition of Interest in Islam: Its Economic Implications and Modes of Interest-free Banking and Finance,* Islamabad: The Third Pak-French Colloquium, 1982, pp. 10-11.

______, *Framework of Islamic Banking, JIBF,* Karachi, (1:2), Spring 1984, pp. 45-50.

ALI, MUAZZAM, *Islamic Banks and Strategies of Economic Cooperation,* London: New Century Publishers, 1982, pp. 120.

Banking Structure and Sources of Finance in the Middle East, London: The Financial Times Business Publishing, 1983, pp. 220.

CHAPRA, M.U., *Towards a Just Monetary System,* Leicester: The Islamic Foundation, 1985, pp. 292.

______ "The Prohibition of Riba in Islam: An Evaluation of Some Objections", *The American Journal of Islamic Studies,* Washington, (2:1), July 1985, pp. 23-40.

Elimination of Interest from the Banking System in Pakistan, Karachi: State Bank of Pakistan, 1985.

HASAN, IBNUL, *In Search of an Islamic Economic Model,* London: New Century Publishers, 1983, pp. 106.

HOMOUD, S.H., *Islamic Banking,* London: Arabian Information, 1985, pp. 300.

KAFF, S.H.A.R., AL-, *Organization of the Credit Operations under the Islamic Banking System,* Karachi: Islamic Research Academy, 1985, pp. 70.

KHAN, M. AKRAM, "Islamic Banking in Pakistan", *International Journal of Islamic and Arabic Studies,* Indiana, (2:2), 1985, pp. 21-34.

KHAN, WAQAR MASOOD, *Towards an Interest-free Islamic Economic System,* Leicester: The Islamic Foundation, 1985, pp. 126.

MEENAI, S.A., "The Problem of Riba" in *Money and Banking in Pakistan,* Karachi: Oxford University Press, 1984, pp. 279-83.

NAQVI, S.N.H., *On Replacing the Institution of Interest in a Dynamic Islamic Economy,* Islamabad: Pakistan Institute of Development Economics, 1981, pp. 45.

NIENHAUS, V., "Islamic Economics, Finance and Banking — Theory and Practice" in *Islamic Banking and Finance*, London: Butterworth, 1986, pp. 1-17.

______, "Principles, Problems and Perspective of Islamic Banking", *Intereconomics,* September 1985, pp. 233-38.

PRESLEY, J.R., *Directory of Islamic Financial Institutions,* London: Croom-Helm, 1988, pp. 360.

SALEH, NABIL A., *Unlawful Gain and Legitimate Profit in Islamic Law,* London: Cambridge University Press, 1986, pp. 130.

SIDDIQI, M.N., *Issues in Islamic Banking,* Leicester: The Islamic Foundation, 1983, pp. 152.

SIDDIQI, M.N., "Monetary Theory of Islamic Economics" in *Issues in Islamic Banking*, Leicester: The Islamic Foundation, 1983, pp. 125-132.

ZAIDI, N.A., "Islamic Banking: Perspective and Problems", *JIBF,* Karachi, (1:3), July 1984, pp. 55-64.

ZAIDI, N.A., "An Alternative Model of Islamic Banking", *JIBF,* Karachi, (1:4), October 1984, pp. 27-38.

Islamic Stock Exchange

CHAPRA, M.U., "The Role of the Stock Exchange in an Islamic Economy", *JRIE,* Jeddah, (3:1), 1985, pp. 75-82.

KHAN, M. AKRAM, "Commodity Exchange and Stock Exchange in Islamic Economy", *AJISS,* Herndon, (5:1), 1988, pp. 91-114.

METAWALLY, M.M., "The Role of the Stock Exchange in an Islamic Economy", *JRIE,* Jeddah, (2:1), Summer 1984, pp. 21-30.

QURESHI, D.M., "The Role of Stock Exchange in Islamic Financial System", *JIBF,* Karachi, (5:3), July 1988, pp. 9-19.

Investment Appraisal

KAFF, S.H.A.R., AL-, *Does Islam Assign any Value/Weight to Time Factor in Economic and Financial Transactions?* Karachi: Islamic Research Academy, 1986, pp. 116.

______, "Investment Leading to Ownership", *Universal Message,* Karachi, (4:10), March 1983, pp. 10-20.

______, "Islamisation of Credit Card Business", *Universal Message,* Karachi, (7:4), Sept 1985, pp. 15-27.

Zakāh

ABU-SAUD, M., *Contemporary Zakat,* Cincinnati: Ohio, 1988, pp. 208.

BASAR, HASMET, *Management and Development of Awqaf Properties,* Jeddah: Islamic Research and Training Institute, 1987, pp. 161.

HASAN, NAJMUL, *Social Security of Islam with Special Reference to Zakah,* Jeddah: ICRIE, 1984, pp. 57.

IMTIAZI, I. A., MANNAN, M. A. NIAZ, and M.A. DERIA, A.H., *Management of Zakah in Modern Muslim Society,* Jeddah: IRTI, 1989, pp. 236.

IQBAL, MUNAWAR; and KHAN, M.F., *Fiscal Policy and Resource Allocation in Islam,* Islamabad: Institute of Policy Studies, 1983, pp. 385.

ISHAQUE, K. M., "Islamic System of Taxation", *Pakistan & Gulf Economist,* Karachi, (4:17), April 1985, pp. 23-26.

OSMAN, M. FATHI, *The Juristic Rules of Conquered Land and Land Taxation: Fay' and Kharāj. Their Origins and Development in Medieval Islam. Unpublished.,* 1976, pp. 626.

SIDDIQI, M. N., *Insurance in an Islamic Economy,* Leicester: The Islamic Foundation, 1985.

TABATABAI, HOSSEIN M., *Kharāj in Islamic Law,* London: Anchor Press, 1983, pp. 276.

Economic Cooperation

ABDELMONEIM, M., "UNIDO Activities in Developing Countries" in Muazzam Ali (ed.), *Islamic Banks and Strategies of Economic Cooperation,* London: New Century Publishers, 1982, pp. 32-36.

AHMAD, ZIAUDDIN, *Role of Islamic Banks in the Economic Integration of the Muslim World. Unpublished.*, October 1986, pp. 15.

ATAS, S.FARID, AL-", An Islamic Common Market and Economic Development, *Islamic Culture*, Hyderabad, (LXI : 1), January 1987, pp. 28-38.

AWAN, K.R., *Prospects for Cooperation through Trade Among OIC Member Countries*, Jeddah: IRTI, 1985,

CARIKCI, EMIN, *Comments on V. Nienhaus's 'Economic Development through Regional Cooperation: A CDU of Islamic Countries. Unpublished,* July 1986, pp. 15.

CHOUDHURY, M.A., "Resource Endowment and Allocation in Islamic Countries for Economic Cooperation", *Orient:. German Journal for Politics & Economics of Middle East,* Opladen, (29:4), 1988, pp. 32-36.

CINDORUK, S., "International Economic Integration and Prospects for an Islamic Common Market", *JIBF,* Karachi, (5:1), Jan. 1988, pp. 113-18.

"Financial Cooperation among Islamic Countries", *Cooperation*, (III/2:10), January 1982, pp. 9-27.

GAYE, A. KARIM, "The Muslim World and the International Economic Perspective " in *The Muslim World and the Future Economic Order,* London: Islamic Council of Europe, 1979, pp. 6-12.

HUQ, ATAUL, *Economic Integration as a Strategy of Development of the Muslim Countries under the Islamic Framework, (typescript),* Nigeria: Sokoto University, February 1985, pp. 38.

KEMAL, A.R., *Comments on V. Nienhaus's 'Economic Development through Regional Cooperation: A CDU of Islamic Countries'. (typescript)* , July 1986, pp. 6.

KHAN, TUFAIL AHMAD, "Economic Integration of Islamic States", *Pakistan Horizon,* Karachi, (1:1), 1983, pp. 29-43.

MATIN, A., "Industrial Cooperation Among Muslim States", *Science and Technology in the Muslim World,* Islamabad, (1:1), January-March 1983, pp. 1-19.

MOINUDDIN, HASAN, *The Charter of the Islamic Conference and Legal Framework of Economic Cooperation among its Member States,* Oxford: Clarendon Press, 1987, pp. 322.

NIENHAUS, V., *Economic Development through Regional Cooperation: A Customs Drawback Union of Islamic Countries,* Islamabad: I.I.I.E., July 1986.

NASSER, EL-GHARIB, "The Role of Islamic Banks for Initiating an Islamic Common Market", *JIBF,* Karachi, (5:1), January 1988, pp. 32.

NIENHAUS, V., "Inter-Islamic Economic Cooperation and Integration" in Erol Manisali (ed.), *Outward Oriented Policies in NIC*, Istanbul: Granti Bankasi, 1986, pp. 51-65.

_____, "An Islamic Common Market: Problems and Strategies of Economic Cooperation among Islamic Countries", *Economics,* Tubingen, (35), 1987, pp. 21-41.

______, *Economic Cooperation and Integration among Islamic Countries : International Framework and Economic Problems*, Jeddah: IRTI, 1987, pp. 163.

SHALABY, I., "The Islamic Common Market", *JIBF,* Karachi, (5:1), January 1983, pp. 83-111.

Economics of Profit and Loss Sharing

ASHKER, A.A.F., AL-, *The Islamic Business Enterprise,* London: Croom-Helm, 1987, pp. 242.

HASAN, ZUBAIR, "Determination of Profit and Loss Sharing Ratios in Interest-free Business Finance", *JRIE,* Jeddáh (3:1), 1985, pp. 13-29.

KARSTEN, INGO, "Islam and Financial Intermediation, *IMF Staff Papers,* Washington, March, 1982, pp. 108-142.

KHAN, S. RAFI, *Profit and Loss Sharing,* Karachi: Oxford University Press, 1987, pp. 180.

NIENHAUS, V., "Islamic Banking: Micro-economic Instruments and Macro-economic Implications", *Arab Banker,* London, (6), November-December 1986, pp. 5-7, 29-39.

QURESHI, D.M., "Mudaraba and its Modern Applications", *JIBF*, Karachi, (2:1), January 1985, pp. 7-24.

SIDDIQI, M.N., *Partnership and Profit-Sharing in Islamic Law,* Leicester: The Islamic Foundation, 1985, pp. 110.

ZAMAN, M. RAQUIBUZ, "Business Organizations and the Instruments for Raising Financial Capital for a Modern Islamic Economy", *Islamic Culture,* Hyderabad, (LX:3), 1986, pp. 1-20.

Accountability

BADAWI, S.T., "Accounting Policies and Procedures" in *Islamic Banking and Finance,* London: Butterworth, 1986, pp. 86-100.

IBN TAYMIYAH, *Public Duties in Islam*, tr. M. Holland, Leicester: The Islamic Foundation, 1982, pp. 160.

KHAN, M. AKRAM, "Role of the Auditor in an Islamic Economy", *JRIE,* Jeddah, (3:1), 1985, pp. 31-42.

SARDAR, Z., *Science, Technology and Development in the Muslim World,* London: Croom Helm, 1977, pp. 215.

TOMKINS, C., ABDUL KARIM, R.A., "The *Sharī'ah* and its Implications for Islamic Financial Analysis", *AJISS,* Washington, (4:1), 1987, pp. 101-115.

WILSON, R., *Islamic Business (Special Report No. 178)*, London: The Economist Intelligence Unit, 1984, pp. 75.

SUBJECT INDEX

U

V

W

Z

GENERAL INDEX

IIIT ENGLISH PUBLICATIONS

A. Islamization of Knowledge Series

- *The Islamic Theory of International Relations: New Directions for Islamic Methodology and Thought:* (1407/1987) by 'Abdul Ḥamīd AbūSulaymān.
- *Islamization of Knowledge: General Principles and Work Plan*, 3rd edition (1409/1989). [A German edition was published under the title *Das Einbringen des Islam in das Wissen* (1408/1988)].
- *Toward Islamic Anthropology: Definitions, Dogma, and Directions* (1406/1986) by Akbar S. Aḥmad.
- *Toward Islamic English* (1406/1986) by Ismā'īl Rājī al Fārūqī. [A German edition was published under the title: *Fürein Islamisches Deutsch* (1408/1988)].
- *Modelling Interest-Free Economy: A Study in Microeconomics and Development* (1407/1987) by Muhammad Anwar.
- *Islam: Source and Purpose of Knowledge*: Papers presented to the Second International Conference of Islamic Thought and the Islamization of Knowledge (1409/1988).
- *Toward Islamization of Disciplines*: Papers presented to the Third International on Islamic Thought and the Islamization of Knowledge (1409/1988).
- *The Organization of the Islamic Conference: An Introduction to an Islamic Political Institution* (1408/1988) by 'Abdullāh al Aḥsan.

- *Proceedings of the Lunar Calendar Conference:* Papers presented to the Conference of the Lunar Calendar. Edited by 'Imād ad-Deen Aḥmad (1408/1988).

- *Islamization of Attitudes and Practices in Science and Technology*: Papers presented to a special seminar on the same topic (1409/1989). Edited by M.A.K. Lodhi.

- *Where East Meets West: The West on the Agenda of the Islamic Revival* (1412/1992) by Mona Abul-Fadl.

- *Qur'ānic Concepts of Human Psyche:* Papers presented to a special seminar organized by IIIT (Pakistan) (1412/1992). Edited by Zafar Afaq Ansari.

- *Islam and the Economic Challenge:* by M. Umer Chapra (1412/1992) Published jointly with the Islamic Foundation (U.K.).

- *Resource Mobilization and Investment in an Islamic Economic Framework*: Papers presented to the 3rd International Islamic Economics Seminar (1412/1991). Edited by Zaidi Sattar.

- *Islam and Economic Development: A strategy for Development with Justice and Stability* By M. Umer Chapra (1414/1993). Publisshed jointly with the Islamic Reserach Istitute (Pakistan).

B. Issues in Contemporary Islamic Thought Series

- *Islamic Thought and Culture*: Papers presented to the Islamic Studies Group of the American Academy of Religion (1402/1982). Edited by Ismā'īl Rājī al Fārūqī.

- *Trialogue of the Abrahamic Faiths*, 2nd edition (1406/1986). Papers presented to the Islamic Studies Group of the American Academy of Religion. Edited by Ismā'īl Rājī al Fārūqī.

- *Islamic Awakening: Between Rejection and Extremism* by Yūsuf al Qaraḍāwī.

- *Madīnan Society at the Time of the Prophet* (1411/1991) by Akram Ḍiyā' al 'Umarī.

    Volume I: *Its Characteristics and Organization.*
    Volume II: *The Jihād Against the Mushrikūn.*

- *Tawḥīd: Its Implications for Thought and Life* (second edition, 1412/1992) by Ismā'īl Rājī al Fārūqī.

C. Research Monographs Series

- *Source Methodology in Islamic Jurisprudence (Uṣūl al Fīqh Islāmī)* (third edition, 1413/1993) by Ṭāhā Jābir al 'Alwānī.

- *Islam and the Middle East: The Aesthetics of a Political Inquiry* (1411/1990) by Mona Abul-Fadl.

- *Sources of Scientific Knowledge: The Concept of Mountains in the Qur'ān* (1411/1991) by Zaghloul R. El-Naggar.

- *Indexation of Financial Assets: An Islamic Evaluation* (1414/1993) by S.M. Hasanuz Zaman.

D. Occasional Papers Series

- *Outlines of a Cultural Strategy* (1410/1989) by Ṭāhā Jābir al 'Alwānī. [A French edition was published under the title *Pour une Strategie Culturelle Islamique* (1411/1990), and a German edition was published under the title *Entwurf Eines Alternativen Kulture Planes* (1413/1992)].

- *Islamization of Knowledge: A Methodology* (1412/1991) by 'Imād al Dīn Khalil [A French edition was published under the title *Methodologie pour Islamization du Savior* (1412-1991)].

- *The Qur'ān and the Sunnah: The Time — Space Factor* (1412/1991) by Tāhā Jābir al 'Alwānī and 'Imād al Dīn Khalīl. [A French edition was published under the title *Le Coran et la Sunna: Le Facteur Tems-Espace* (1412/1992).

- *Knowledge: An Islamic Perspective* (1412/1991) by Bakhtiar Ḥusain Siddiqui.

- *Islamization of Knowledge: A Critical Overview* (1413/1992) by Seyyed Vali Reza Nasr.

- *Ijtihad* (1413/1993) by Ṭāhā Jābir al Ālwānī

E. Human Development Series

- *Training Guide for Islamic Workers* by Hisham Altalib, (second revised edition 1412-1992). [Turkish and Malay editions were published in (1412/1992)].

F. **Perspectives on Islamic Thought Series**

- *National Security and Development Strategy* (1412-1991) by Arshad Zaman.

- *Nationalism and Internationalism in Liberalism, Marxism and Islam* (1412/1991) by Tahir Amin.

G. **Islamic Methodology Series**

- *Crisis in the Muslim Mind* (1414/1993) by 'AbdulHamīd A. Abūsulaymn.

H. **Academic Dissertations**

- *Through Muslim Eyses:* M. Rashid Riḍā and the west

Journals

- *American Journal of Islamic Social Sciences* (AJISS). Quarterly published jointly with the Association of Muslim Social Scientists (AMSS), U.S.A.

- *Muslim World Book Review* and *Index of Islamic Literature*. Quarterly published jointly with the Islamic Foundation (U.K.)